Mike McGrath

jQuery

In easy steps is an imprint of In Easy Steps Limited
16 Hamilton Terrace · Holly Walk · Leamington Spa
Warwickshire · United Kingdom · CV32 4LY
www.ineasysteps.com

Notice of Liability
Every effort has been made to ensure that this book contains accurate
and current information. However, In Easy Steps Limited and the
author shall not be liable for any loss or damage suffered by readers
as a result of any information contained herein.

Trademarks
All trademarks are acknowledged as belonging to their respective
companies.

In Easy Steps Limited supports The Forest Stewardship Council (FSC),
the leading international forest certification organisation. All our titles
that are printed on Greenpeace approved FSC certified paper carry the
FSC logo.

MIX
Paper from
responsible sources
FSC® C020837

Printed and bound in the United Kingdom

ISBN 978-1-84078-619-4

Contents

Preface

The creation of this book has been for me, Mike McGrath, an exciting opportunity to build upon the scripting examples demonstrated in the companion book "JavaScript in easy steps". Employing the jQuery JavaScript library lets you easily create dynamic interactive functionality. Example code listed in this book describes how to produce jQuery functionality in easy steps – and the screenshots illustrate the actual results. I sincerely hope you enjoy discovering the exciting possibilities of jQuery and have as much fun with it as I did in writing this book.

In order to clarify the code listed in the steps given in each example I have adopted certain colorization conventions. Components of the JavaScript language are generally colored blue, HTML code and literal values are black, and comments are green. Additionally, in an attempt to readily identify HTML components selected by a jQuery object, those components are colored red – both in the listed HTML code and in the listed JavaScript code, like this:

```
<p> <button id = "btn" > Send AJAX Request </button> </p>

$( document ).ready( function() {
  $( "#btn" ).on( "click" , function() {
  // AJAX request to be added here.
  } ) ;
) } ;
```

In order to identify each source code file described in the steps a colored icon and a file name appears in the margin alongside the steps:

page.html   plugin.js   parser.php   product.txt

For convenience I have placed source code files from the examples featured in this book into a single ZIP archive. You can obtain the complete archive by following these three easy steps:

1. Open a web browser and navigate to **www.ineasysteps.com** then select the "Free Resources" menu and choose the "Downloads" item

2. Next find "jQuery in easy steps" in the list then click on the hyperlink entitled "All Code Examples" to download the archive

3. Now extract the contents to any convenient location, such as your Desktop, and copy all contents of the **htdocs** sub-folder into your web server's documents directory

1 Getting started

Welcome to the exciting world of jQuery scripting for dynamic web pages. This chapter introduces the jQuery library and demonstrates how to select HTML elements.

Introducing jQuery

jQuery is a lightweight multi-browser JavaScript library that is designed to make it easier to incorporate JavaScript features on websites. The library provides methods that can be called with just a single line of code to achieve results that would otherwise require many lines of JavaScript – so you can "write less, do more".

jQuery is free open-source software that was first released back in 2006 by its original author John Resig, but is now maintained by the jQuery Team of developers. The library is currently used by over 65% of the 10,000 most-visited websites and is the most popular JavaScript library in use today.

jQuery's syntax is designed to make it easy to select components of a web page for the purposes of:

- Manipulation of HTML/DOM elements

- Modification of CSS style rules

- Attachment of event handlers to respond to user actions

- Creation of dynamic effects and animations

- Development of interactive AJAX applications

jQuery also allows developers to create their own plugins on top of the standard JavaScript library to suit specific requirements. These may provide anything from a simple, small utility to a complex widget or an advanced animation. This modular approach to the jQuery library enables the creation of powerful dynamic web pages and web applications.

Don't forget

JavaScript is a client-side scripting language whereas jQuery is a library written in the JavaScript language.

jQuery is supported by the Adobe Dreamweaver web development application and by the Microsoft Visual Studio Express For Web development application for use within the ASP.NET AJAX and ASP.NET MVC frameworks. Both applications have an "Intellisense" feature that recognizes jQuery syntax and provides coding hints. This feature is very useful but it is not at all essential – all the examples in this book are easily created in a plain text editor, such as Windows' Notepad application.

Enabling jQuery

The entire jQuery library is contained in a single JavaScript file that may be freely downloaded from **jquery.com/download** Compressed and uncompressed copies of the jQuery library file are available for download. There are no functional differences between these files but the uncompressed copy is formatted with spacing and comments, to make it easily human-readable, whereas the compressed copy is minimized by the removal of spacing and comments – to reduce the file size and so improve performance. Unless you wish to examine the source code of the jQuery library itself you should download the compressed copy and place it in the directory containing your HTML web page documents.

In order to enable the jQuery library to be used on your web pages the jQuery library file must be incorporated into the web page by including an HTML **<script>** tag within the head section of the HTML document to indicate the jQuery library's location.

The minimized jQuery library is a file named something like **jquery-1.11.0.min.js**, describing the current version number, and can be enabled in your web page by including these HTML tags in the head section of your web page:

```
<script src="jquery-1.11.0.min.js"> </script>
```

There are also 2.x.x versions of the jQuery library file that are further minimized by removal of support for older web browsers. As an alternative to hosting a copy of the jQuery library alongside your web pages you can indicate the jQuery library's location online at the Google CDN (Content Delivery Network) like this:

```
<script
   src="//ajax.googleapis.com/ajax/libs/jquery/1.11.0/jquery.min.js">
</script>
```

or at the Microsoft CDN (Content Delivery Network) like this:

```
<script
   src="//ajax.aspnetcdn.com/ajax/jQuery/jquery-1.11.0.min.js">
</script>
```

As jQuery is so popular many users may already have downloaded the library file from Google or Microsoft into their browser's cache when visiting another site. This means it can quickly be loaded from cache when they visit your site.

Hot tip

jQuery resolves multi-browser issues automatically – it performs identically in all major browsers, including Internet Explorer 6.

Beware

Change the version number in the tag to match that of the jQuery library file you download or indicate online.

Recognizing readiness

Having enabled jQuery to be used on your web page, as described on the previous page, you can add a second **<script>** element to the head section to contain statements calling jQuery functions. Each jQuery statement typically contains a "selector", to select one or more HTML elements of the document, and an "action" to be performed on that selection. The statement syntax looks like this:

$(*selector*).*action*( ) ;

The **$( )** function queries the HTML document to find the elements specified by the selector then returns a jQuery object that is a collection of those matched elements. Dot notation is then used to append the action to be performed on the elements.

A comprehensive collection of elements specified by a selector cannot be accurately retrieved until the HTML document has loaded and its Document Object Model (DOM) has been built. At this point a "document ready" event gets fired in the browser to signal that the document is ready for manipulation by jQuery.

Readiness of the document can be recognized by specifying the document's own **document** object as the selector and calling the **ready()** action function when the "document ready" event fires.

It is good practice to specify an anonymous JavaScript function within the parentheses of the **ready()** action function whose statements can be executed safe in the knowledge that all elements are available. The complete code block looks like this:

```
<script>

$( document ).ready( function() {

// Statements to be executed when the document is ready.

} ) ;

</script>
```

Every example in this book places statements within the body of this anonymous JavaScript function to ensure the document is completely loaded before attempting to manipulate its content. The HTML5 document listed opposite makes the jQuery library available then simply produces an alert dialog indicating readiness.

Don't forget

It is not necessary to include a **type** attribute in the **<script>** tag for HTML5 documents.

```
< !DOCTYPE HTML >
< html lang = "en" >
< head >
< meta charset = "UTF-8" >
< title >jQuery Ready Function< /title >

< script src = "jquery-1.11.0.min.js" >< /script >

< script >

$( document ).ready(  function() {

  alert( "Hello World!" ) ;

} ) ;

< /script >
< /head >
< body >
< h1 >jQuery< /h1 >
<!-- Elements to be added here. -->
< /body >
< /html >
```

ready.html

11

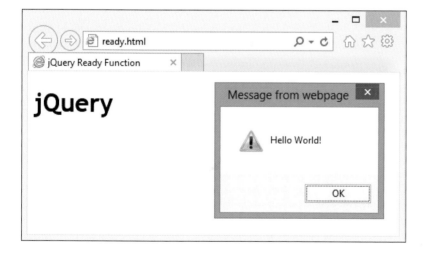

As all statements are always wrapped inside the call to the **$(document).ready()** function jQuery also allows this shorter alternative syntax to be used if you prefer it:

$(function() {

// Statements to be executed when the document is ready.

}) ;

Avoiding conflict

The "$" character that is used by jQuery syntax is also used by other JavaScript libraries such as MooTools, Backbone and JavaScriptMVC. It is therefore possible for conflicts to arise between calls to jQuery functions and those of another library.

Fortunately the **$()** function syntax is merely a shortcut to the actual library function **jQuery()** which may be used directly instead. Additionally, the jQuery library provides a **jQuery.noConflict()** method that removes the shortcut ability of the "$" character so conflicts between libraries can be avoided:

noconflict.html

1 In the head section of an HTML document begin a script block with a call to remove the **$()** shortcut ability **jQuery.noConflict() ;**

2 Next, add a direct call to recognize the "document ready" event by producing an alert dialog message **jQuery(document).ready(function() {**

  alert("jQuery Is Working!") ;
}) ;

3 Save the document alongside the jQuery library file then open it in a web browser to see the direct call execute

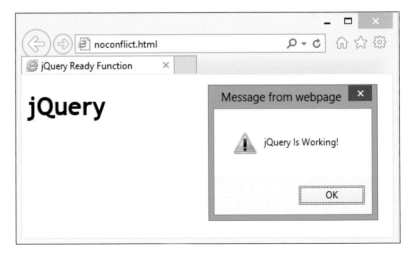

Selecting by tag name

Element Selector

A jQuery selector specifies which elements of the HTML document are to be returned in the jQuery object for manipulation. An Element Selector simply specifies a tag name within quote marks between the selector function's parentheses. For example, the selector call **$("p")** queries the HTML document and returns all **<p>** paragraph elements.

Each selector call can append an action function, using dot notation, to specify an action to perform on the collection of returned elements. For example, the jQuery **text()** method can be appended to specify a text string within quote marks between its parentheses. The specified string will then be written into each matched element, replacing any existing content. This could be used to replace the existing text content of each item in a list:

 Add an ordered list to the body of an HTML document
<ol><li>Item<li>Item<li>Item</ol>

In the head section of the HTML document add a script block that recognizes the "document ready" event by selecting all list item elements and replacing text content
$(document).ready(function() {

  $("li").text("Generated Content") ;
}) ;

Save the document alongside the jQuery library file then open it in a browser to see the generated list item content

tagname.html

Don't forget

Only specify the tag name to the selector – angled markup brackets are not required.

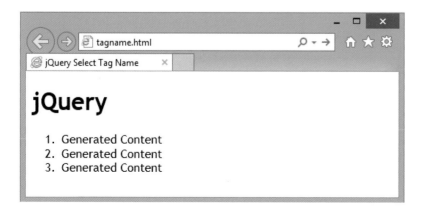

jQuery

1. Generated Content
2. Generated Content
3. Generated Content

Selecting by ID and class

ID Selector

A jQuery selector can specify a particular element by its identity. An ID Selector specifies the unique value of an element that has been assigned to its **id** attribute. This must be prefixed by a **#** hash character and enclosed within quote marks between the selector function's parentheses. For example, a selector **$("#two")** queries the HTML document and returns the element that has the value "two" assigned to its **id** attribute. An identity selector call can append an action function, using dot notation, to specify an action to perform on the returned element:

identity.html

1. Add an ordered list to the body of an HTML document
```
<ol>
<li id = "one" >ID Item
<li id = "two" >ID Item
<li id = "three" >ID Item
</ol>
```

2. In the head section of the HTML document add a script block that recognizes the "document ready" event by selecting one list item element and replacing text content
```
$( document ).ready( function() {

  $( "#two" ).text( "Generated Content" ) ;
} ) ;
```

3. Save the document alongside the jQuery library file then open it in a browser to see the generated list item content

Class Selector

A jQuery Class Selector can also return a collection of elements of a particular class by specifying the value assigned to their **class** attribute. This should be prefixed by the element name followed by a . period character, and the whole expression enclosed within quote marks between the selector function's parentheses. For example, the selector **$("li.rest")** queries the HTML document and returns the list item elements that have the value "rest" assigned to their **class** attribute. A class selector call can append an action function, using dot notation, to specify an action to perform on the returned elements:

1. Add an ordered list to the body of an HTML document
```
<ol>
<li class = "start" >Class Item
<li class = "rest" >Class Item
<li class = "rest" >Class Item
</ol>
```

class.html

2. In the head section of the HTML document add a script block that recognizes the "document ready" event by selecting list item elements and replacing text content
```
$( document ).ready( function() {

  $( "li.rest" ).text( "Generated Content" ) ;
} ) ;
```

3. Save the document alongside the jQuery library file then open it in a browser to see the generated list item content

Don't forget

Internally, element selectors use the **getElementsByTagName()** DOM method and class selectors use the **getElementsByClassName()** DOM method.

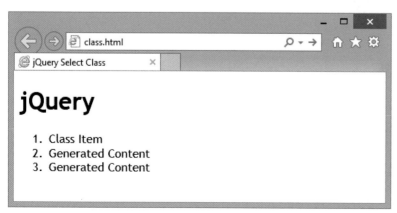

Selecting attributes and order

Attribute selector

A jQuery selector can specify elements by attribute name or by attribute name and value. An "Has Attribute" selector selects all elements having an attribute name specified in [ ] brackets within double quote marks between the selector function's parentheses. For example, **$("[lang]")** returns all elements that have a "lang" attribute. An "Equals" selector also specifies an attribute value – enclosed within single quote marks to differentiate it from the outer double quotes. For example, **$("[lang='fr']")** returns all elements that have the value "fr" assigned to their "lang" attribute. Attribute selector calls can append a method, using dot notation, to specify an action to perform on the returned elements:

attribute.html

1   Add an ordered list to the body of an HTML document
```
<ol>
<li lang = "fr" >Attribute Item
<li lang = "fr" >Attribute Item
<li lang = "en" >Attribute Item
</ol>
```

2   In the head section of the HTML document add a script block that recognizes the "document ready" event by selecting list item elements and replacing text content
```
$( document ).ready( function() {

  $( "[lang='fr']" ).text( "Generated Content" ) ;
} ) ;
```

3   Save the document alongside the jQuery library file then open it in a browser to see the generated list item content

Hot tip

The selector can prefix the attribute by a tag name to select only elements of a certain type having the specified attribute. For example, **$("p[lang]")** returns only paragraph elements that have a **lang** attribute.

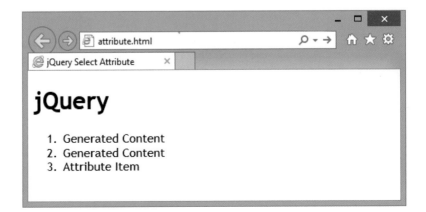

attribute.html

jQuery Select Attribute

jQuery

1. Generated Content
2. Generated Content
3. Attribute Item

16

Filter selector

A jQuery selector can also return elements according to their zero-based index position in a selection. The element name can be suffixed by **:first** or **:last** "filters" to select a single element. Alternatively, the filters **:odd** or **:even** can be used to select a subset. An individual element can also be selected by specifying its index number within the brackets of an **:eq( )** filter. Subsets of the collection can be selected above and below a specified index position by specifying that index number within the brackets of **:gt( )** or **:lt( )** filters. For example, a selector **$("li:lt(2)")** queries the HTML document and returns the first and second elements. An order selector call can append an action method, using dot notation, to specify an action to perform on returned elements:

Hot tip

The **:odd** filter can be used to stripe table rows.

1   Add an unordered list to the body of an HTML document
```
<ul>
<li>Even Item 0<li>Odd Item 1<li>Even Item 2
</ul>
```

order.html

2   In the head section of the HTML document add a script block that recognizes the "document ready" event by selecting list item elements and replacing text content
```
$( document ).ready( function() {

  $( "li:even" ).text( "Generated Content" ) ;
} ) ;
```

3   Save the document alongside the jQuery library file then open it in a browser to see the generated list item content

Don't forget

Index numbering begins at zero and is considered to be an even number.

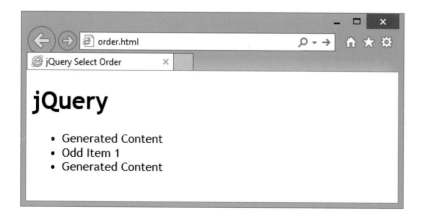

jQuery

- Generated Content
- Odd Item 1
- Generated Content

Selecting family relatives

Descendant selector

A jQuery selector can return elements according to their relationship to another element using a "Descendant" selector to specify the outer parent element name followed by a space and the name of an inner descendant element. For example, the selector **$("p span")** queries the HTML document and returns all span elements within each paragraph of the document. Descendant selector calls can append an action method, using dot notation, to specify an action to perform on returned elements:

descendant.html

1 Add an ordered list to the body of an HTML document
```
<ol>
<li>Descendant Item
<li>Descendant <span>Item</span>
<li>Descendant Item
</ol>
```

2 In the head section of the HTML document add a script block that recognizes the "document ready" event by selecting a span element and replacing its text content
```
$( document ).ready( function() {

  $( "ol span" ).text( "Generated Content" ) ;
} ) ;
```

3 Save the document alongside the jQuery library file then open it in a browser to see the generated span content

Don't forget

Descendant selectors select immediate child elements and other hierarchy levels too, such as grandchild elements.

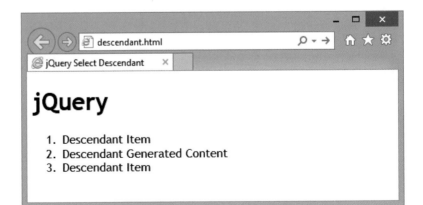

Child selector

All child elements of a specified parent element can be selected using a "Child" selector stating the parent name followed by a ">" character and the child name. For example, a selector $("ol > li") selects all list items in each ordered list of the HTML document.

Child filter selector

A jQuery selector can also specify elements by their relationship to other elements using a Child Filter specifying the name of a child element followed by a **:first-child** or **:last-child** filter to select a single child of each parent element. For example, a selector $("li:first-child") selects the first child list item element within each list of the HTML document. Child selectors and selectors with Child Filters can append a method, using dot notation, to specify an action to perform on the returned elements:

 Add an ordered list to the body of an HTML document
```
<ol><li>Child Item<li>Child Item<li>Child Item</ol>
```

2 In the head section of the HTML document add a script block that recognizes the "document ready" event by selecting a list item element and replacing its text content
```
$( document ).ready( function() {

  $( "li:last-child" ).text( "Generated Content" ) ;
} ) ;
```

3 Save the document alongside the jQuery library file then open it in a browser to see the generated list item content

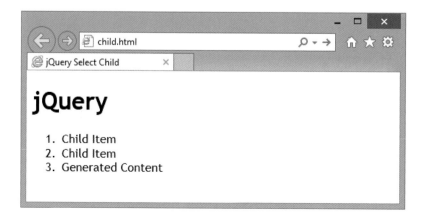

Selecting multiple elements

Multiple selector

A jQuery selector can be combined with another to create a specific selection expression. For example, an identity selector that targets a particular list in an HTML document can be combined with an "Order" selector that targets a particular item in that list. Additionally, multiple selection expressions can appear in a single jQuery selector as a comma-separated list. Each multiple selector can append an action method, using dot notation, to specify an action to perform on all the returned elements:

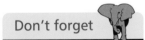

multiple.html

1 Add two ordered lists to the body of an HTML document, each with a unique identity
```
<ol id = "list1" >
<li>List Item<li>List Item<li>List Item</ol>
<ol id = "list2" >
<li>List Item<li>List Item<li>List Item</ol>
```

2 In the head section of the HTML document add a script block that recognizes the "document ready" event by selecting an item in each list and replacing text content
```
$( document ).ready( function() {

$( "#list1 li:eq(1) , #list2 li:eq(2)" ).text( "Generated Content" ) ;
} ) ;
```

3 Save the document alongside the jQuery library file then open it in a browser to see the generated list item content

Don't forget

Index numbering begins at zero so the second item in a list is at index position one.

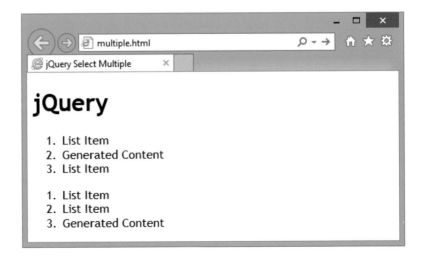

All selector

In jQuery the * asterisk character is a wildcard that can be used in a **$("*")** universal "All" selector to select all elements in an HTML document. Perhaps more usefully, it can also be used with the jQuery **find()** method to select all descendants of a specified element. For example, a selector **$("body").find("*")** queries the HTML document and returns all elements within the document body. The returned collection can be assigned to a variable, creating an array, and a loop can be used to reveal each tag name:

1 Add a paragraph containing a span after the heading in the body of an HTML document
```
<h1>jQuery</h1>
<p>Output: <span id = "out" ></span></p>
```

universal.html

2 In the head section of the HTML document add a script block that recognizes the "document ready" event by first initializing counter, string, and array variables
```
$( document ).ready( function() {

  var i = 0 , str = "" , elements = $( "body" ).find( "*" ) ;
} ) ;
```

3 Next, in the script block, add a loop to build a string of retrieved tag names then display that string in the span
```
for( ; i < elements.length ; i++ )
{ str += ( elements[ i ].tagName + " | " ) } ;
$( "#out" ).text( str + elements.length ) ;
```

4 Save the document alongside the jQuery library file then open it in a browser to see the generated span content

Beware

The jQuery documentation warns that the * universal selector is "extremely slow, except when used by itself".

Filtering visibility

Visibility filter selector

A jQuery selector can filter out elements from a returned collection according to their visibility on the page by specifying **:visible** or **:hidden** filters to the jQuery **filter()** method. Only elements that have styles of **display:none**, form elements of **type="hidden"**, elements whose width and height are set to zero, or who are descendants of any of these, are regarded as hidden. For example, a selector **$("body").find("*").filter(":hidden")** returns all truly hidden elements within the document body:

hidden.html

 Add a hidden division with bold text and a paragraph containing a span in the body of an HTML document
```
<div style="display:none"><b>Hidden Text</b></div>
<p>Output: <span id = "out" ></span></p>
```

2 In the head section of the HTML document add a script block that recognizes the "document ready" event by first initializing counter, string, and array variables
```
$( document ).ready( function() {

    var i = 0 , str = "Hidden: " ;
    var hid = $( "body" ).find( "*" ).filter( ":hidden" ) ;
} ) ;
```

3 Next, in the script block, add a loop to build a string of hidden tag names then display that string in the span
```
for( ; i < hid.length ; i++ )
{ str += ( hid[ i ].tagName + " | " ) } ;
$( "#out" ).text( str + hid.length ) ;
```

  Save the document alongside the jQuery library file then open it in a browser to see the generated span content

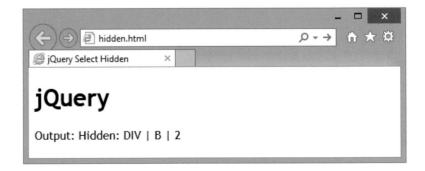

22

Optimizing selections

Examples on the previous pages demonstrate various ways to select a collection of elements with jQuery but some consideration should be given to selector efficiency:

- **Select by identity where possible** – HTML **id** attributes are unique in each page so even older browsers find the element quickly. Ideally use $("#theIdentity") format for each selector.

- **Select with both element and class** – when selecting by **class** older browsers examine every element on the page unless the selector gives an element name to limit the search. Use $("p.theClass") format rather than $(".theClass")

- **Select in the simplest way** – avoid unnecessary complexity. A complex selector $("body article.topic p#theIdentity em") can simply use $("#theIdentity em") instead as the **id** is unique anyway so including its ancestors is unnecessary.

- **Select from right to left** – jQuery selects from right to left so it loads all right-most matches into an array before discarding those that do not match those to the left in the selector. A selector $("#theIdentity em") loads all document **em** elements before discarding those not matching **#theIdentity"**. For optimum efficiency use $("#theIdentity").find("em")

- **Select only once** – avoid repetition of selections like these
  $("p").text("Generated Content") ;
  $("p").css("color" , "red") ;
  "Chaining" can apply multiple methods in one statement.
  Use $("p").text("Generated Content").css("color" , "red") ;
  Assign the jQuery object to a variable if you need to reference it more than once like the statement in the example opposite
  var hid = $("body").find("*").filter(":hidden") ;
  Then, use **hid.length** and **hid[i].tagName** as often as required.

Summary

- jQuery is a lightweight multi-browser JavaScript library that makes it easier to incorporate JavaScript features on websites

- jQuery can be enabled by hosting the minimized jQuery library file on your website or alternatively by indicating the library file's location online at the Google or Microsoft CDN

- A jQuery statement typically contains a selector to return a collection of elements and an action to be performed on them

- The **$(document).ready( )** function gets called when the DOM has loaded and so can usefully contain an anonymous JavaScript function enclosing all jQuery statements

- The **$( )** function syntax is a shortcut for the **jQuery( )** function that can be used instead, and if using **jQuery.noConflict()**

- jQuery's most basic selectors specify elements by tag name **$("p")**, by identity **$("#theId")**, and by class **$("p.theClass")**

- jQuery Attribute selectors select all elements containing a set attribute **$("[lang]")** or those of set value **$("[lang='fr']")**

- jQuery Order selectors select elements according to their zero-based index position in a selected collection **$("li:eq(1)")**

- jQuery Child selectors select only all immediate children of a specified parent element, but not grandchildren **$("ol > li")**

- jQuery Descendant selectors select all hierarchy levels below a specified parent element, including grandchildren **$("p span")**

- Multiple selection expressions can appear in a single jQuery selector as a comma-separated list

- The * universal selector can be used with the **find()** method to select all descendants of an element **$("body").find("*")**

- Elements can be selected according to visibility with the **filter()** method **$("body").find("*").filter(":hidden")**

2 Performing actions

This chapter demonstrates how to specify a subset of elements from a selected collection and how to manipulate CSS styles.

Traversing elements

A collection of selected elements returned in a jQuery object can be iterated over, looping in turn, by the object's **each()** method. The element of the current iteration can, usefully, be referenced using the jQuery **this** keyword to apply an action to that element.

Internally, the **each()** method maintains an index number count of the current loop iteration, which can be appended to the content of each element in the collection:

each.html

1　Add an unordered list to the body of an HTML document, with common list item content
```
<ul>
<li>List Item<li>List Item<li>List Item
</ul>
```

2　In the head section of the HTML document add a script block that selects all items in the list and appends a space and an index number to each list item
```
$( document ).ready( function() {

  $( "li" ).each( function( index ) {

    $( this ).text( $( this ).html() + " " + index ) ;
  } );

} ) ;
```

3　Save the document alongside the jQuery library file then open it in a browser to see the appended list item content

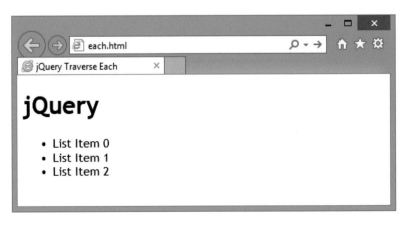

A collection of selected elements returned in a jQuery object can be reduced to simply reference only the first matched element using the object's **first()** method. Similarly, a collection of selected elements can be reduced to reference only the last matched element using that jQuery object's **last()** method.

When manipulating an identical collection of elements more than once, a single selection statement can best assign the collection to a variable. That jQuery object's methods can then be called on the variable without repeating the selection process:

1 Add an unordered list to the body of an HTML document, with common list item content
<ul> <li>Item<li>Item<li>Item </ul>

first.html

2 In the head section of the HTML document add a script block that assigns a collection of all list items to a variable
$(document).ready(function() {

  var items = $("li") ;

}) ;

3 Now, add statements in the script block to reduce the collection and modify each single referenced element
items.first().text("First Item") ;
items.last().text("Last Item") ;

4 Save the document alongside the jQuery library file then open it in a browser to see the modified list item content

Don't forget

It is efficient and good practice to assign a jQuery object to a variable to avoid repeatedly selecting the same element collection.

27

Moving along

Elements in a document's DOM tree can be referenced by moving along the DOM tree from an initial jQuery selection. The sibling immediately following the element matched in a jQuery object can be referenced using that object's **next()** method. Similarly, the previous sibling of the element matched in a jQuery object can be referenced using that object's **prev()** method:

next.html

1 Add an ordered list to the body of an HTML document, with unique list item identities but common content
```
<ol>    <li id = "item1" >Item
        <li id = "item2" >Item
        <li id = "item3" >Item
        <li id = "item4" >Item
        <li id = "item5" >Item  </ol>
```

2 In the head section of the HTML document add a script block that selects the first list item and modifies the next list item's content
```
$( document ).ready( function() {

  $( "#item1" ).next().text( "Generated Text" ) ;

} ) ;
```

3 Now, add a statement in the script block that selects the last list item and modifies the previous list item's content
```
$( "#item5" ).prev().text( "Generated Text" ) ;
```

Hot tip

Optionally, the **next()** and **prev()** methods can accept a selector argument to further test whether the sibling element should match.

4 Save the document alongside the jQuery library file then open it in a browser to see the modified list item content

Multiple elements in a document's DOM tree can be referenced by moving along the DOM tree from an initial jQuery selection using that object's **nextUntil()** method. This selects all following sibling elements until, but not including, that specified by the method's argument. Alternatively, all following sibling elements can be selected using the jQuery object's **nextAll()** method.

Similarly, the jQuery object's **prevUntil()** method selects all previous sibling elements until, but not including, that specified by the method's argument. Alternatively, all previous sibling elements can be selected using the jQuery object's **prevAll()** method:

1 Add an ordered list to the body of an HTML document, with unique list item identities but common content

```
<ol>    <li id = "item1" >Item
        <li id = "item2" >Item
        <li id = "item3" >Item
        <li id = "item4" >Item
        <li id = "item5" >Item  </ol>
```

until.html

2 In the head section of the HTML document add a script block that modifies three sibling list items' content

```
$( document ).ready( function() {

    var collection = $( "#item1" ).nextUntil( $( "#item5" ) ) ;
    collection.text( "Generated Text" ) ;
} ) ;
```

3 Save the document alongside the jQuery library file then open it in a browser to see the modified list item content

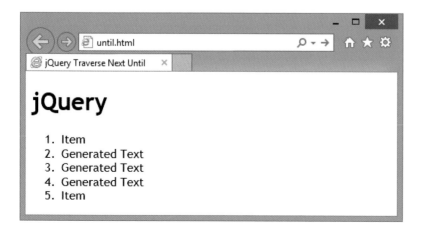

Don't forget

Remember that the **nextUntil()** and **prevUntil()** methods match siblings up to the specified element, but do not include that element.

Visiting relatives

Elements in a document's DOM tree can be referenced by relationship to a jQuery selection. All immediate "child" descendants of the selection can be referenced using that object's **children()** method. Additionally, all adjacent siblings of a selection can be referenced using the jQuery object's **siblings()** method. Optionally, the **children()** and **siblings()** methods may specify a selector argument to further filter the elements to be referenced:

children.html

 Add an unordered list and an ordered list to the body of an HTML document
```
<ul><li>Son<li>Son<li>Son</ul>
<ol><li>Daughter<li>Daughter<li>Daughter</ol>
```

2 In the head section of the HTML document add a script block that selects the unordered list and modifies the text of each its child list items
```
$( document ).ready( function() {

  $( "ul" ).children().text( "Child" ) ;
} ) ;
```

3 Now, add a statement in the script block that selects the first ordered list item and modifies its sibling list items
```
$( "ol li:first-child" ).siblings().text( "Sibling" ) ;
```

4 Save the document alongside the jQuery library file then open it in a browser to see the modified list item content

Beware

The **children()** method only travels a single level down the DOM tree – use the **find()** method to travel down multiple levels, as on page 21.

Parent elements in a document's DOM tree can be referenced by relationship to a jQuery selection. The immediate "parent" ancestor of the selection can be referenced using that object's **parent()** method. Additionally, that and all higher ancestor levels of a selection can be referenced using the jQuery object's **parents()** method. Optionally, **parent()** and **parents()** methods may specify a selector argument to further filter the elements to be referenced:

① Add a division, containing a paragraph with emphasized text and a paragraph with a span, to the body of an HTML document

```
<div>
<p>Paragraph containing <em>Emphatic Text</em></p>
<p>Output: <span id="out"></span></p>    </div>
```

parents.html

② In the head section of the HTML document add a script block that initializes counter, string, and array variables

```
$( document ).ready( function() {

  var i = 0 , str = "", parents = $( "em" ).parents() ;
} ) ;
```

③ Next, in the script block, add a loop to build a string of parent tag names then display the string in the span

```
for( ; i < parents.length ; i++ )
{ str += parents[ i ].tagName + " | " } ;
$( "#out" ).text( str + parents.length ) ;
```

④ Save the document alongside the jQuery library file then open it in a browser to see the generated span content

Hot tip

Note **$("html").parent()** returns a jQuery object containing **document** but **$("html").parents()** returns an empty set.

31

Interrogating selections

Elements returned in a jQuery collection can be interrogated to discover whether the collection contains at least one specified element among their descendants. The element to seek must be specified as an argument to the jQuery object's **has()** method.

A jQuery collection may also be interrogated to discover whether any contained element is itself a specified element. In this case the element to seek must be specified as an argument to the jQuery object's **is()** method. Where the specified element IS found, this method returns **true**, otherwise it returns **false**:

interrogate.html

1   Add an ordered list containing a span and a paragraph containing a span to the body of an HTML document
```
<ol><li>Item<li><span>Item</span><li>Item</ol>
<p>Output: <span id = "out" ></span></p>
```

2   In the head section of the HTML document add a script block that modifies the text of the span in the list item
```
$( document ).ready( function() {

  $( "li" ).has( "span" ).text( "Item : Has Span" ) ;
} ) ;
```

3   Now, add a statement in the script block that outputs a confirmation only if the list is an ordered list type
```
if( $( "li" ).parent().is( "ol" ) )
{ $( "#out" ).text( "This Is An Ordered List" ) ; }
```

4   Save the document alongside the jQuery library file then open it in a browser to see the modified list item content

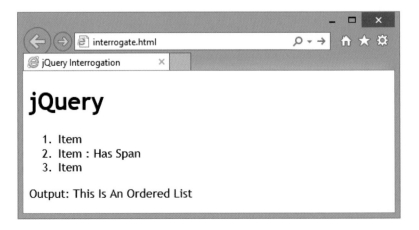

Elements returned in a jQuery collection can be interrogated to discover whether they do NOT contain at least one specified element among their descendants. The element to seek must be specified as an argument to the jQuery object's **not()** method. Whereas the **has()** method creates a new jQuery object containing only successfully matched elements, the **not()** method creates a new jQuery object containing only elements not matched:

1 Add an unordered list containing a span and a paragraph containing a span to the body of an HTML document
```
<ul><li>Item<li><span>Item</span><li>Item</ul>
<p>Output: <span id = "out" ></span></p>
```

not.html

2 In the head section of the HTML document add a script block that modifies the list items without a span
```
$( document ).ready( function() {

  var nospan = $( "li" ).not( $( "li" ).has( "span" ) ) ;
  nospan.text( "Item : Has No Span" ) ;
} ) ;
```

3 Now, add a statement in the script block that outputs a confirmation only if the list is an unordered list type
```
if( $( "li" ).parent().not( "ol" ) )
{ $( "#out" ).text( "This Is An Unordered List" ) ; }
```

4 Save the document alongside the jQuery library file then open it in a browser to see the modified list item content and list type confirmation

Hot tip

Notice that the element to seek can be specified by its tag name or as a jQuery selector.

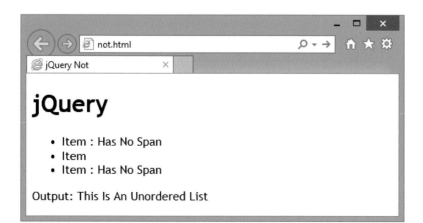

33

Applying styles

Style property values of the first matched element returned in a jQuery collection can be retrieved using that jQuery object's **css()** method. The name of the property whose value is to be retrieved must be supplied as an argument enclosed within quote marks to the **css()** method. Color values are typically returned in "rgb" notation, so that a red value is rgb(255 , 0 , 0):

getproperty.html

1. Add an ordered list and a paragraph containing a span to the body of an HTML document
   `<ol><li>Alpha<li>Bravo<li>Charlie</ol>`
   `<p>Output: <span id = "out" ></span></p>`

2. In the head section of the HTML document add a simple style sheet to color the list contents red
   `<style> ol { color : red ; } </style>`

3. Next, in the head section of the HTML document, add a script block that gets the current list color property value
   `$( document ).ready( function() {`

   `$( "#out" ).text( $( "ol" ).css( "color" ) ) ;`
   `} ) ;`

4. Save the document alongside the jQuery library file then open it in a browser to see the value of the list color displayed in the span

Don't forget

The style sheet could alternatively specify the red color as **#FF0000** or **rgb(255,0,0)** – but the retrieved color value will always be output in **rgb()** notation format.

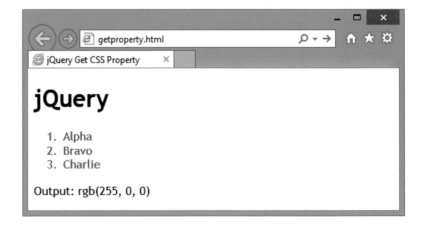

Style property values of an element returned in a jQuery object can be set using that jQuery object's **css()** method. The name of the property to be set and its value must be enclosed within quote marks and supplied as a comma-separated argument pair to the **css()** method. Color values may be specified using a recognized name, hexadecimal notation, or rgb notation. For example, the color value "blue", "#0000FF", or "rgb(0 , 0 , 255)":

① Add an ordered list to the body of an HTML document
```
<ol id = "list" ><li>Alpha<li>Bravo<li>Charlie</ol>
```

HTML

setproperty.html

② In the head section of the HTML document add a script block that stores the list jQuery object in a variable
```
$( document ).ready( function() {

  var list = $( "#list" ) ;
} ) ;
```

③ Now, add statements in the script block that set the width and colors of the list
```
list.css( "background-color" , "blue" ) ;
list.css( "color" , "yellow" ) ;
list.css( "width" , "300" ) ;
```

④ Save the document alongside the jQuery library file then open it in a browser to see the list styles applied

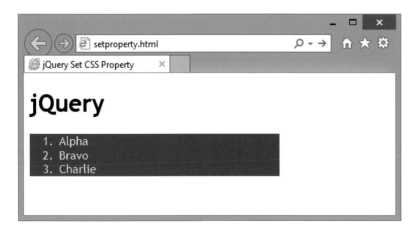

Hot tip

Notice that the width value "300" does not need an explicit "px" suffix as pixel units are automatically assumed.

35

Adding values

Multiple styles of an element in a jQuery object can be set in a single statement using JavaScript Object Notation (JSON). Each property name and its desired value must be enclosed within quote marks and separated by a : colon character to form a name:value pair. A comma-separated list of these name:value pairs can then be enclosed within { } braces to create a complete JavaScript "object". Styles are applied by specifying the JavaScript object as an argument to the jQuery object's **css()** method:

object.html

1 Add an ordered list to the body of an HTML document
   `<ol><li>Alpha<li>Bravo<li>Charlie</ol>`

2 In the head section of the HTML document add a script block that sets the width and colors of the list

```
$( document ).ready( function() {

  $( "ol" ).css(
    { "background-color" : "blue" ,
      "color" : "yellow" ,
      "width" : "300"
    }
  ) ;

} ) ;
```

3 Save the document alongside the jQuery library file then open it in a browser to see the list styles applied

As an alternative to adding styles to an element returned in a jQuery object with the **css()** method, styles can be applied by adding a class to the element – defining one or more styles. The name of the class to be added must be specified as an argument enclosed within quote marks to the jQuery object's **addClass()** method. Multiple classes can be added to an element with a single statement by specifying their names as a space-separated argument list to the **addClass()** method:

 Add an ordered list to the body of an HTML document
`<ol><li>Xray<li>Yankee<li>Zulu</ol>`

2 In the head section of the HTML document add a style sheet to specify width and color classes
```
<style>
.W300 { width : 300px ; }
.yelFG { color : yellow ; }
.redBG { background : red ; }
</style>
```

3 Next, in the head section of the HTML document, add a script block that adds each class to the list
```
$( document ).ready( function() {

  $( "ol" ).addClass( "W300 yelFG redBG" ) ;
} ) ;
```

4 Save the document alongside the jQuery library file then open it in a browser to see the class styles applied

addclass.html

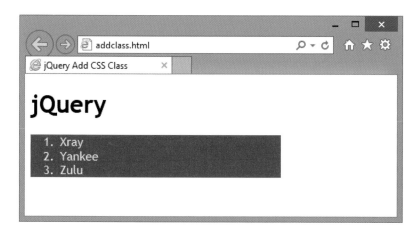

Beware

The **addClass()** method does not replace classes but merely adds classes – appending them to any which may already be assigned to the element.

Toggling classes

A style class applied to elements returned in a jQuery object can be switched (toggled) using that object's **toggleClass()** method. The name of the class must be specified as an argument enclosed within quote marks to the jQuery object's **toggleClass()** method. Where an element already has that style class it will be removed, otherwise the class will be added to that element. Additionally, the jQuery object's **hasClass()** method can be used to confirm whether an element has a specified style class:

toggleclass.html

1 Add an unordered list and a paragraph containing a span with a class attribute to the body of an HTML document
```
<ul><li>Item<li>Item<li>Item</ul>
<p>Output: <span class="grnBG" id="out"></span></p>
```

2 In the head section of the HTML document add a simple style sheet to specify a color and width class
```
<style>
.grnBG   { background: green ; color: white ; width: 300px ; }
</style>
```

3 Next, in the head section of the HTML document, add a script block that toggles and confirms the class attribute
```
$( document ).ready( function() {

  $( "span , ul" ).toggleClass( "grnBG" ) ;
  $( "#out" ).text( $( "span" ).hasClass( "grnBG" ) ) ;
} ) ;
```

Don't forget

The **hasClass()** method returns a Boolean value of **true** or **false** – to indicate whether the specified element has the specified class.

4 Save the document alongside the jQuery library file then open it in a browser to see the class styles toggled

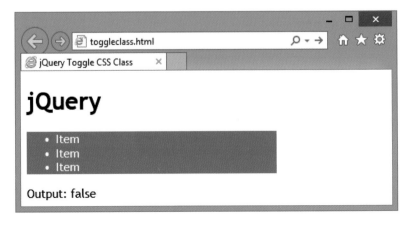

A class applied to an element returned in a jQuery object can be removed by specifying the class name as an argument enclosed within quote marks to the jQuery object's **removeClass()** method. Typically, this is used to exchange one class applied to the selected element for another class by "chaining" a call to the **removeClass()** method with a call to the **addClass()** method in a single statement:

1. Add an unordered list with a class and a paragraph containing a span to the body of an HTML document
```
<ul class="grnBG"><li>Item<li>Item<li>Item</ul>
<p>Output: <span id = "out" ></span></p>
```

removeclass.html

2. In the head section of the HTML document add a style sheet to specify two color and width classes
```
<style>
.grnBG   { background: green ; color: white ; width: 300px ; }
.yelBG   { background: yellow ; color : blue ; width: 300px ; }
</style>
```

3. Next, in the head section of the HTML document, add a script block that removes one class and adds another, then confirms the class attribute
```
$( document ).ready( function() {

  $( "ul" ).removeClass( "grnBG" ).addClass( "yelBG" ) ;
  $( "#out" ).text( $( "ul" ).hasClass( "yelBG" ) ) ;
} ) ;
```

4. Save the document alongside the jQuery library file then open it in a browser to see the class styles exchanged

Hot tip

The technique of "chaining" method calls is good practice in jQuery scripting as it performs multiple actions with a single statement.

Calculating sizes

The dimensions of a box element returned in a jQuery object can be retrieved using that jQuery object's **width()** and **height()** methods. These return the numeric pixel size value, without a "px" suffix. Alternatively, the value can be retrieved to include the suffix using that object's **css("width")** and **css("height")** methods:

size.html

1. Add a division and two paragraphs each containing a span to the body of an HTML document
```
<div id = "box" >Box</div>
<p>Box Width : <span id = "w" ></span>
<br>Box Height: <span id = "h" ></span> </p>
```

2. In the head section of the HTML document add a style sheet to specify rules for the division
```
<style>
#box { width: 200px  ; height: 50px ;
background: yellow ; padding: 5px ; border: 5px solid red ; }
</style>
```

3. Next, in the head section of the HTML document add a script block that displays the box dimensions
```
$( document ).ready( function() {
  var box = $( "#box" ) ;
  $( "#w" ).text( box.width() + " or " + box.css( "width" ) ) ;
  $( "#h" ).text( box.height() + " or " + box.css( "height" ) ) ;
} ) ;
```

4. Save the document alongside the jQuery library file then open it in a browser to see the box width and height

Don't forget

The **width()** and **height()** methods return the pixel size of the box excluding any padding or margin.

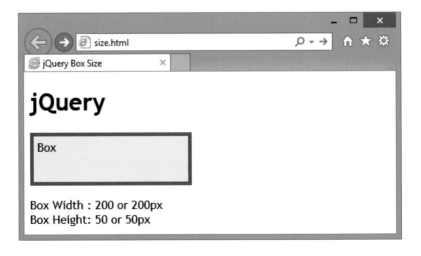

The overall dimensions of a box element returned in a jQuery object can be retrieved using that jQuery object's **innerWidth()** and **innerHeight()** methods, to include padding, or using **outerWidth()** and **outerHeight()** methods to include both padding and margins:

 Add a division and a paragraph containing a span to the body of an HTML document
```
<div id="box">Box</div>
<p>Output: <span id = "out" ></span></p>
```

In the head section of the HTML document add a style sheet to specify rules for the division
```
<style>
#box    { width: 200px ; height: 50px ;
background: yellow ; padding: 5px ; border: 5px solid red ; }
</style>
```

Next, in the head section of the HTML document, add a script block that displays the overall box sizes
```
$( document ).ready( function() {
  var box = $( "#box" ) , str = "Including Padding - " ;
  str += box.innerWidth() + "x" + box.innerHeight() ;
  str += "<br>Including Padding & Margin- " ;
  str += box.outerWidth() + "x" + box.outerHeight() ;
  $( "#out" ).html( str ) ;
} ) ;
```

Save the document alongside the jQuery library file then open it in a browser to see the overall box dimensions

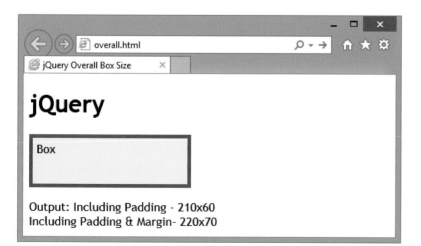

overall.html

Hot tip

You can use the **height()** and **width()** methods of **$(window)** and **$(document)** jQuery objects to get the browser viewport and document dimensions.

41

Beware

The **innerWidth()**, **outerWidth()**, **innerHeight()**, and **outerHeight()** methods each return a numeric pixel value without a "px" suffix.

Summary

- Elements in a jQuery object can be iterated over using the object's **each()** method and the element on the current iteration can be referenced using the **this** keyword

- The first element in a collection can be referenced by the **first()** method and the last element by the **last()** method

- Following elements in the DOM tree can be referenced by the **next()**, **nextUntil()**, or **nextAll()** methods and previous elements by the **prev()**, **prevUntil()**, or **prevAll()** methods

- Relative elements in the DOM tree can be referenced using **children()**, **siblings()**, **parent()**, or **parents()** methods

- A specified element can be sought in a jQuery collection by the **has()** method, by the **is()** method, or by the **not()** method

- A style property value of an element in a jQuery object can be retrieved or set using that object's **css()** method

- Multiple styles of an element can be set when specified as a JavaScript (JSON) object argument to the **css()** method

- One or more classes can be added to an element in a jQuery object using that object's **addClass()** method and may be removed using that object's **removeClass()** method

- A style class applied to an element can be switched (toggled) using its jQuery object's **toggleClass()** method

- A specified class can be sought in the element within a jQuery object by using that object's **hasClass()** method

- The dimensions of a box element, without padding or margin, can be retrieved in numeric format using its jQuery object's **width()** and **height()** methods

- Overall dimensions of a box element, including padding and margin, can be retrieved in numeric format using its jQuery object's **outerWidth()** and **outerHeight()** methods

3 Managing forms

This chapter demonstrates how to select HTML form elements for manipulation and form submission.

Selecting text fields

HTML form elements can best be selected for a jQuery object by identifying their input **type** attribute. For example, all text field form elements of **<input type="text">** can be selected with the selector **$("input[type='text']")**. Each element in the returned collection can be referenced by its index number using that jQuery object's **eq()** method and its associated value retrieved by chaining a **val()** method onto the statement:

textfield.html

1 Add a form containing text fields and a paragraph containing a span to the body of an HTML document
```
<form>
<input type="text" name = "user" value = "Mike" >
<input type="text" name = "addr" value = "Broadway" >
<input type="text" name = "city" value = "New York" >
</form> <p>Output: <span id = "out" ></span></p>
```

Don't forget

Collection index numbering begins at zero not 1.

2 In the head section of the HTML document add a script block that selects all text fields and displays the first value
```
$( document ).ready( function() {

    var user = $( "input[type='text']" ).eq( 0 ).val() ;
    $( "#out" ).text( user ) ;
} ) ;
```

3 Now, add a statement in the script block to replace the value in the first selected text field
```
$( "input[type='text']" ).eq( 0 ).val( "Replaced Content" ) ;
```

Hot tip

There is also a jQuery text field selector of **$(input:text)** but using **$("input[type='text']")** is the preferred method for better performance.

4 Save the document alongside the jQuery library file then open it in a browser to see the text field values

```
textfield.html

jQuery Select Text Input

jQuery

[Replaced Content]  [Broadway]  [New York]

Output: Mike
```

Unlike text fields, which are created with an **<input>** tag, text area elements, created with a **<textarea>** tag, do not contain a **type** attribute – so can be selected for a jQuery object using their tag name and **name** attribute together with its assigned value. Values for the text area element selected in a jQuery object can be inserted or retrieved by that object's **val()** method:

1 Add a form containing a text area and a paragraph containing a span to the body of an HTML document

```
<form>
<textarea name = "content" rows = "3" cols = "50" >
</textarea>
</form>
<p>Output: <span id = "out" ></span></p>
```

textarea.html

2 In the head section of the HTML document add a script block that selects the text area and inserts a value

```
$( document ).ready( function() {

  var content = $( "textarea[name='content']" ) ;
  content.val( "Text Area Content" ) ;
} ) ;
```

3 Now, add a statement in the script block to display the value that has been inserted into the text area

```
$( "#out" ).text( content.val() ) ;
```

4 Save the document alongside the jQuery library file then open it in a browser to see the text area values

Hot tip

Password text fields are simply text inputs of the password type so can be selected using **$(input[type='password'])**

45

Selecting by ability

The value of a property in a jQuery object can be retrieved by specifying the desired property name as an argument to that object's **prop()** method. Additionally, the property value can be set by specifying the desired value as a second argument to the **prop()** method. This can be used to determine whether a form element is disabled or can set an enabled element to become disabled:

disabled.html

1 Add a form containing three text inputs and a paragraph containing a span to the body of an HTML document
```
<form>
<input type="text" name = "A" value = "Alpha" >
<input type="text" name = "B" value = "Bravo" >
<input type="text" name="C" value="Charlie"></form>
<p>Output: <span id = "out" ></span></p>
```

2 In the head section of the HTML document add a script block that disables the third text input
```
$( document ).ready( function() {

    var box3 = $( "input[type='text']" ).eq( 2 ) ;
    box3.prop( "disabled" , true ) ;
} ) ;
```

3 Now, add a statement in the script block to display a confirmation if the third text input is disabled
```
if( box3.prop( "disabled" ) === true )
{ $( "#out" ).text( box3.val() + " Disabled" ) ; }
```

Beware

Do not use the jQuery **removeProp()** method to remove **disabled** or **checked** properties, as once removed they cannot be added again later – use the **prop()** method to set these properties to **false** instead as shown here.

4 Save the document alongside the jQuery library file then open it in a browser to see the disabled text input field

← →	disabled.html	⌕ → ⌂ ★ ⚙
jQuery Select Disabled ×		

jQuery

Alpha	Bravo	Charlie

Output: Charlie Disabled

Form elements that contain a **disabled** attribute are by default disabled so the user cannot enter input there. Any disabled form element selected in a jQuery object can be enabled by specifying the disabled property name within quote marks as the first argument to that object's **prop()** method and the keyword **false** as its second argument:

1 Add a form of three disabled text inputs and a paragraph containing a span to the body of an HTML document

```
<form>
<input type="text" name="A" value="Alpha" disabled >
<input type="text" name="B" value="Bravo" disabled >
<input type="text" name="C" value="Charlie" disabled >
</form> <p>Output: <span id = "out" ></span></p>
```

enabled.html

2 In the head section of the HTML document add a script block that enables the third text input

```
$( document ).ready( function() {

  var box3 = $( "input[type='text']" ).eq( 2 ) ;
  box3.prop( "disabled" , false ) ;
} ) ;
```

3 Now, add a statement in the script block to display a confirmation if the third text input is disabled

```
if( box3.prop( "disabled" ) === false )
{ $( "#out" ).text( box3.val() + " Enabled" ) ; }
```

4 Save the document alongside the jQuery library file then open it in a browser to see the enabled text input field

47

Hot tip

Use the **prop()** method to get and set **disabled** and **checked** property values but use the **val()** method to get and set all other attribute values.

Selecting radio buttons

The status of a form's radio button element in a jQuery object can be retrieved by specifying the **checked** property name as an argument to that object's **prop()** method. This will return a **true** value if that radio button is checked, otherwise it will return **false**. Status can be altered by specifying the **checked** property name within quote marks as the first argument to the **prop()** method and a Boolean **true** or **false** value as its second argument:

radio.html

1 Add a form with three radio buttons and a paragraph containing a span to the body of an HTML document

```
<form>
ONE<input type="radio" name = "btn" value = "ONE" >
TWO<input type="radio" name = "btn" value = "TWO" >
THREE<input type="radio" name="btn" value="THREE">
</form> <p>Output: <span id = "out" ></span></p>
```

2 In the head section of the HTML document add a script block that checks the third radio button

```
$( document ).ready( function() {

    var rad3 = $( "input[type='radio']" ).eq( 2 ) ;
    rad3.prop( "checked" , true ) ;
} ) ;
```

3 Now, add a statement in the script block to display a confirmation if the third radio button is checked

```
if( rad3.prop( "checked" ) === true )
{ $( "#out" ).text( rad3.val() + " Checked" ) ; }
```

4 Save the document alongside the jQuery library file then open it in a browser to see the checked radio button

Hot tip

There is also a jQuery radio button selector of **$(input:radio)** but **$("input[type='radio']")** is the preferred method for better performance.

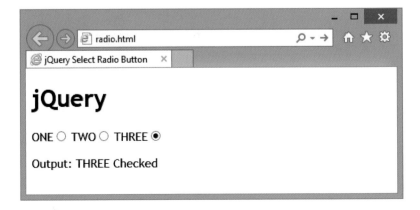

Selecting checkboxes

The status of a form's checkbox input element in a jQuery object can be retrieved by specifying the **checked** property name as an argument to that object's **prop()** method. This will return a **true** value if that checkbox is checked, otherwise it will return **false**. Status can be altered by specifying the **checked** property name within quote marks as the first argument to the **prop()** method and a Boolean **true** or **false** value as its second argument:

1 Add a form containing three checkboxes and a paragraph containing a span to the body of an HTML document
```
<form>
ONE<input type="checkbox" name="box1" value="1">
TWO<input type="checkbox" name="box2" value="2">
THREE<input type="checkbox" name="box3" value="3">
</form> <p>Output: <span id = "out" ></span></p>
```

checkbox.html

2 In the head section of the HTML document add a script block that checks the third checkbox
```
$( document ).ready( function() {

  var chk3 = $( "input[type='checkbox']" ).eq( 2 ) ;
  chk3.prop( "checked" , true ) ;
} ) ;
```

3 Now, add a statement in the script block to display a confirmation if the third checkbox is checked
```
if( chk3.prop( "checked" ) === true )
{ $( "#out" ).text( chk3.val() + " Checked" ) ; }
```

4 Save the document alongside the jQuery library file then open it in a browser to see the checked checkbox

Hot tip

There is also a jQuery checkbox selector of **$(input:checkbox)** but **$("input[type='checkbox']")** is the preferred method for better performance.

Selecting options

The status of a select option element in a jQuery object can be retrieved by specifying the **selected** property name as an argument to that object's **prop()** method. This will return a **true** value if that option is checked, otherwise it will return **false**. Status can be altered by specifying the **selected** property name within quote marks as the first argument to the **prop()** method and a Boolean **true** or **false** value as its second argument:

option.html

1. Add a form containing a select drop-down box with three options and a paragraph containing a span to the body of an HTML document
```
<form> <select>
<option value="ONE">ONE <option value="TWO">TWO
<option value="THREE">THREE </select> </form>
<p>Output: <span id = "out" ></span></p>
```

2. In the head section of the HTML document add a script block that selects the third option
```
$( document ).ready( function() {

    var opt3 = $( "option[value='THREE']" ) ;
    opt3.prop( "selected" , true ) ;
} ) ;
```

3. Now, add a statement in the script block to display a confirmation if the third option is selected
```
if( opt3.prop( "selected" ) === true )
{ $( "#out" ).text( opt3.val() + " Selected" ) ; }
```

4. Save the document alongside the jQuery library file then open it in a browser to see the selected option

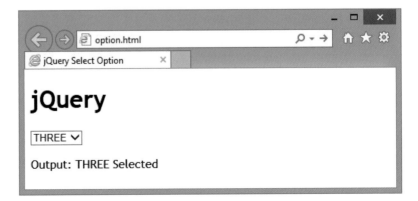

Don't forget

The "selected" property only applies to options – radio buttons and checkboxes use the "checked" property.

When the user selects an option in a select list, a "change event" occurs that can be recognized by the jQuery **change()** method. An anonymous function argument can be specified to this method to provide a change response. The selected option in a collection of option elements within a jQuery object can be determined by specifying a **":selected"** argument to that object's **filter()** method:

1 Add a form containing a select list with three options and a paragraph containing a span to the body of an HTML document

```
<form> <select>
<option value="ONE">ONE <option value="TWO">TWO
<option value="THREE">THREE </select> </form>
<p>Output: <span id = "out" ></span></p>
```

change.html

2 In the head section of the HTML document add a script block that recognizes changes in the select list

```
$( document ).ready( function() {

  $( "select" ).change(
    // Anonymous function to be inserted here.
  ) ;
} ) ;
```

Beware

Notice that the argument to the **filter()** method must be **":selected"** – beginning with a semi-colon character.

3 Now, insert an anonymous function argument in the script block to display a confirmation of the option selected

```
function() { var pick = $( "option" ).filter( ":selected" ) ;
        $( "#out" ).text( pick.val() + " Selected" ) ; }
```

4 Save the document alongside the jQuery library file then open it in a browser to see the selected option

Hot tip

There is also a jQuery option selector of $("option:selected") but $("option").filter(":selected") is the preferred method for better performance.

Selecting buttons

Form button input elements can best be selected for a jQuery object by identifying their input **type** attribute. For example, all form input button elements of **<input type="button">**. Additionally, **<button>** elements can also be selected by their element name. A multiple jQuery selector can specify both to ensure that all buttons get selected in a collection:

button.html

1 Add a form, containing a regular input button and an element button, together with a paragraph containing a span to the body of an HTML document

```
<form>
<input type="button" value = "Regular Button" >
<button>Element Button</button>
</form>
<p>Output: <span id = "out" ></span></p>
```

2 In the head section of the HTML document add a script block that selects all buttons

```
$( document ).ready( function() {

    var btns = $( "input[type='button'] , button" ) ;
} ) ;
```

3 Now, add statements in the script block to add a border to each button and display the number of selected buttons

```
btns.css( "border" , "3px solid red" ) ;
$( "#out" ).text( btns.length + " Buttons Selected" ) ;
```

4 Save the document alongside the jQuery library file then open it in a browser to see the selected buttons

Hot tip

There is also a jQuery input button selector of **$(input:button)** but **$("input[type='button']")** is the preferred method for better performance.

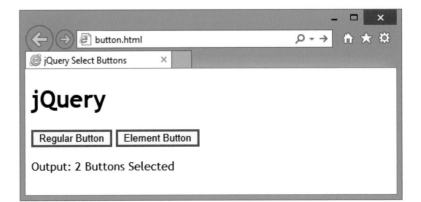

Form button input elements that are other than regular button types can also be selected for a jQuery object by identifying their **type** attribute. For example, all form reset button elements with **<input type="reset">**. A multiple jQuery selector can specify each type to have non-regular buttons selected in a collection:

1. Add a form containing regular, reset, and submit buttons together with a paragraph containing a span to the body of an HTML document

```
<form>
<input type="button" value="Regular Button">
<input type="reset" value = "Reset Button" >
<input type="submit" value = "Submit Button" >
</form> <p>Output: <span id = "out" ></span></p>
```

reset.html

2. In the head section of the HTML document add a script block that selects the non-regular buttons

```
$( document ).ready( function() {

    var btns = $( "input[type='reset'] , input[type='submit']" ) ;
} ) ;
```

3. Now, add statements in the script block to add a border to each selected button and display the number selected

```
btns.css( "border" , "3px solid red" ) ;
$( "#out" ).text( btns.length + " Buttons Selected" ) ;
```

4. Save the document alongside the jQuery library file then open it in a browser to see the selected buttons

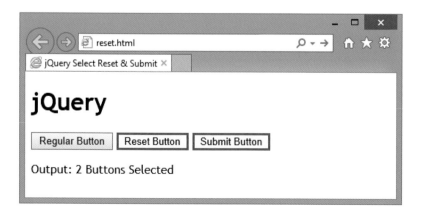

Hot tip

There are also jQuery input selectors of $("input:reset") and $("input:submit"), but type attribute selection is the preferred method for better performance.

Selecting file inputs

Form file input elements can best be selected for a jQuery object by identifying their input **type** attribute. When the user selects a file, a "change event" occurs that can be recognized by the jQuery **change()** method. An anonymous function argument can be specified to this method to provide a change response. The selected file address can be retrieved by that object's **val()** method:

1 Add a form containing a file input and a paragraph containing a span to the body of an HTML document

```
<form enctype="multipart/form-data"
                method="POST" action="file.php">
<input type="file" name = "userfile" size = "50" >
<input type="submit" >
</form>
<p>Output: <span id = "out" ></span></p>
```

file.html

2 In the head section of the HTML document add a script block that recognizes changes in the file input

```
$( document ).ready( function() {

  $( "input[type='file']" ).change(
    // Anonymous function to be inserted here.
  ) ;
} ) ;
```

3 Now, insert an anonymous function argument in the script block to display a confirmation of the file selected

```
function() { $( "#out" ).text( $( this ).val() ) ; }
```

4 Save the document alongside the jQuery library file then open it in a browser to see the selected file

jQuery Select File Input

jQuery

E:\tick.svg   Browse...

Output: E:\tick.svg

Form image input elements can best be selected for a jQuery object by identifying their input **type** attribute. A value can be assigned to the image input by specifying a string argument to the object's **val()** method and also retrieved by its **val()** method:

① Add a form containing an image input and a paragraph containing a span to the body of an HTML document
```
<form>
<input type="image" src="tick.png" alt="Action" >
</form>
<p>Output: <span id = "out" ></span></p>
```

image.html

② In the head section of the HTML document add a script block that assigns a value to the image input element
```
$( document ).ready( function() {

  var img = $( "input[type='image']" ) ;
  img.val( "Action Button" ) ;
} ) ;
```

Beware

Don't confuse an **<input type="image">** element with a regular **<img>** element.

③ Now, add a statement in the script block to display the value of the image input element
```
$( "#out" ).text( img.val() ) ;
```

④ Save the document alongside the jQuery library file then open it in a browser to see the assigned value

55

Hot tip

There is also a jQuery image input selector of **$(input:image)** but **$("input[type='image']")** is the preferred method for better performance.

Recognizing focus

When the user selects a form element in a jQuery object for input, a "focus event" occurs that can be recognized by that object's **focus()** method, and when focus moves away from that form element a "blur event" occurs that can be recognized by that object's **blur()** method. An anonymous function argument can be specified to each method to provide a response to each event:

HTML

focus.html

1 Add a form containing two text inputs and a paragraph containing a span to the body of an HTML document

```
<form>
<input type="text" name = "a" value="jQuery" >
<input type="text" name = "b" value = "in easy steps" >
</form> <p>Output: <span id = "out" ></span></p>
```

2 In the head section of the HTML document add a script block that confirms when the first text input gains and loses focus

```
$( document ).ready( function() {

   var txt = $( "input[type='text']" ).eq(0) ;
   var out = $( "#out" ) ;
   txt.focus( function() { out.text( "Active" ) ; } ) ;
   txt.blur ( function() { out.text( "Inactive" ) ; } ) ;
} ) ;
```

Hot tip

Calling the **focus()** method of an element in a jQuery object without any argument places focus on that element.

3 Save the document alongside the jQuery library file then open it in a browser and repeatedly Tab to focus and blur

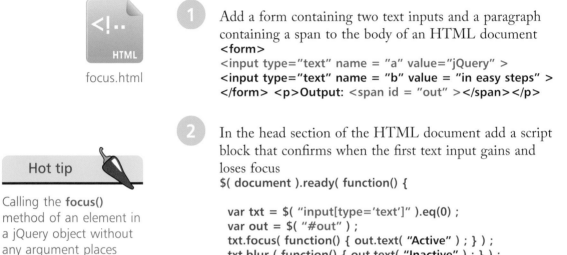

The **focus()** and **blur()** methods recognize when the element itself gains or loses focus. In contrast to this, the **focusin()** and **focusout()** methods recognize when the element itself or any element it contains has focus – which means they support "event bubbling". An anonymous function argument can be specified to each of these methods to provide an appropriate focus response:

1. Add a form containing two text inputs and a paragraph containing a span to the body of an HTML document
```
<form>
<input type="text" name = "a" value = "jQuery" >
<input type="text" name = "b" value = "in easy steps" >
</form>
<p>Output: <span id = "out" ></span></p>
```

focusin.html

2. In the head section of the HTML document add a script block that confirms when any form input has focus
```
$( document ).ready( function() {

  var frm = $( "form" ) ;
  var out = $( "#out" ) ;
  frm.focusin( function() { out.text( "Form Active" ) ; } ) ;
  frm.focusout( function() { out.text( "Form Inactive" ) ; } ) ;
} ) ;
```

Don't forget

In this example, the form will remain "active" when either text input has focus and only become "inactive" when focus moves away.

3. Save the document alongside the jQuery library file then open it in a browser and repeatedly Tab to see focus

Submitting forms

When a form element in a jQuery object gets submitted by the user, a "submit event" occurs that can be recognized by that object's **submit()** method. An anonymous function argument can be specified to confirm validation or that the user does indeed wish to submit the form to the web server for a response:

submit.html

1. Add a form, containing two text inputs and a submit button, together with a paragraph, containing a span, to the body of an HTML document

```
<form action = "submit.php" method = "POST" >
Name: <input type="text" name = "name" >
City: <input type="text" name = "city" >
<br><br><input type="submit"> </form>
<p>Output: <span id = "out" ></span></p>
```

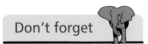

Hot tip

Calling the **submit()** method of a form element in a jQuery object without any argument triggers submission of the form.

2. In the head section of the HTML document add a script block that recognizes when the form gets submitted

```
$( document ).ready( function() {

  $( "form" ).submit(
    // Anonymous function to be inserted here.
  ) ;
} ) ;
```

3. Now, insert an anonymous function argument in the script block to confirm the user does wish to submit the form

```
function() {
  if( confirm( "Submit Form?" ) ) {
    return true ;
  }
  else {
    $( "#out" ).text( "Form Submission Cancelled" ) ;
    return false ;
  }
}
```

Don't forget

This example requires a local web server to be installed along with PHP server support – more details are provided later for AJAX (in chapter 8).

4. Save the document in the documents folder of a web server, alongside the jQuery library file and the nominated response script, then open the document in a browser and submit the form to see the confirmation and the web server response that employs the submitted user input

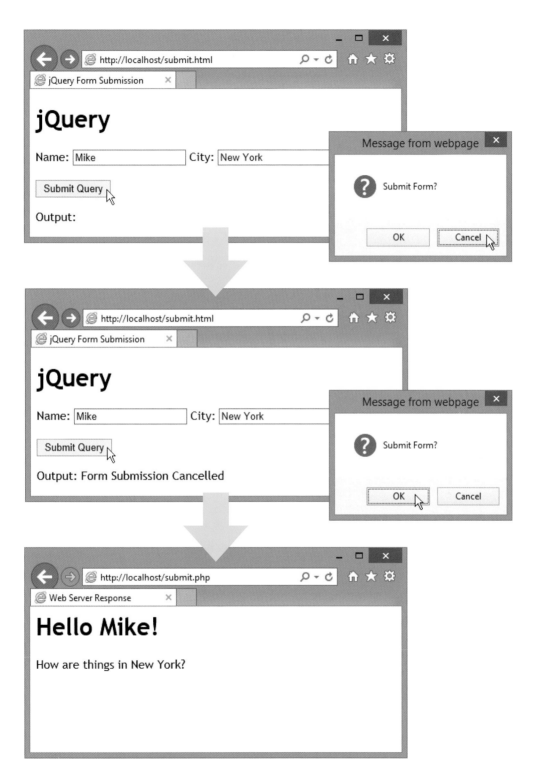

Summary

- Form elements can best be selected for a jQuery object by identifying their **type** attribute

- An input element in a collection can be referenced by stating its index number to the jQuery object's **eq()** method and its value retrieved by chaining the **val()** method to the statement

- Form **<textarea>** elements can be selected for a jQuery object using their tag name and **name** attribute

- A jQuery object's **prop()** method can retrieve the value of a specified property or can set a property with a specified value

- The **disabled, checked,** and **selected** properties return a Boolean **true** value when set, otherwise they return a **false** value

- A "change" event occurs when the user selects a dropdown list option and can be recognized by the jQuery **change()** method

- The currently selected option in a list can be determined by specifying a "**:selected**" argument to the jQuery **filter()** method

- Form input button elements and **<button>** elements can both be selected for a jQuery object using a single multiple selector

- Form input submit, reset, and file types buttons can also be selected for a jQuery object by identifying their **type** attribute

- A "change" event occurs when the user selects a file input and this can be recognized by the jQuery **change()** method

- The "focus" and "blur" events occur as the user selects form elements and can be recognized by **focus()** and **blur()** methods

- Bubbling is supported by the **focusin()** and **focusout()** methods

- A "submit" event occurs when the user submits a form to the server and can be recognized by the jQuery **submit()** method

- All jQuery methods that recognize events can specify an anonymous function to perform an appropriate response

4 Manipulating elements

This chapter demonstrates how to adjust HTML element content and how to attach data to elements.

Changing content

The text content contained between the HTML tags of an element in a jQuery object can be retrieved simply by calling that object's **text()** method, and its existing text can be replaced by specifying new text as a string argument to the **text()** method. Additionally, an anonymous function can be specified as the argument to the **text()** method that will receive the index position and existing text content of the element as its own arguments:

text.html

1 Add two paragraphs containing a span each to the body of an HTML document – with text in the first span only
```
<p>New Text :
<span id = "new" >Java in easy steps</span></p>
<p>Old Text :
<span id = "old" ></span></p>
```

2 In the head section of the HTML document add a script block that references the text content within the first span
```
$( document ).ready( function() {
  $( "#new" ).text(
    // Anonymous function to be inserted here.
  ) ;
} ) ;
```

3 Now, insert an anonymous function argument to copy the text into the second span then replace it with new text
```
function( i , txt ) {
        $( "#old" ).text( txt ) ;
        return "C Programming in easy steps" ; } ) ;
```

Don't forget

The **text()** method cannot be used on form input elements – for input field text you must use the **val()** method.

4 Save the document alongside the jQuery library file then open it in a browser to see the manipulated element text

Unlike the **text()** method, which retrieves only the content contained between an element's HTML tags, calling the **html()** method retrieves both the tags and the content they contain. Complete existing elements can be replaced by specifying new elements as an argument to the **html()** method. Additionally, an anonymous function argument can be specified to receive the index position and existing HTML element as its own arguments:

1 Add an unordered list and a paragraph containing a span to the body of an HTML document
```
<ul><li>Apple<li>Banana<li>Cherry</ul>
<p>Output : <span id = "out" ></span></p>
```

html.html

2 In the head section of the HTML document add a script block that references the list's html and text content
```
$( document ).ready( function() {
  $( "ul" ).html(
    // Anonymous function to be inserted here.
  ) ;
} ) ;
```

3 Now, insert an anonymous function argument to copy the html as text in the span then replace it with new elements
```
function( i , html ) {
        $( "#out" ).text( html ) ;
        return "<li>Damson<li>Elderberry<li>Fig" ; } ) ;
```

4 Save the document alongside the jQuery library file then open it in a browser to see the manipulated element text

63

Beware

The **html()** method uses the browser's **innerHTML** property and may not exactly replicate the original HTML element – notice here that Internet Explorer adds a final closing **</li>** tag.

Changing attributes

The value of an attribute within an element in a jQuery object can be retrieved by specifying the attribute name as an argument to that object's **attr()** method. An attribute value can be set by specifying the attribute name and its desired value as a comma-separated argument pair to the **attr()** method. For example, to set a **width** attribute to a value of 100 with **attr("width" , "100")**. Multiple attributes can be set by creating a JavaScript object of comma-separated name:value pairs enclosed within **{ }** braces:

attr.html

ffox.png

1. Add a paragraph containing an image and a span to the body of an HTML document
```
<p><img src = "ffox.png" alt = "Firefox" >
<br>Output: <span id = "out" ></span></p>
```

2. In the head section of the HTML document add a script block that changes the source and alternative image text
```
$( document ).ready( function() {
  var img = $( "img[ alt = 'Firefox' ]" ) ;
  img.attr( { "src" : "tbird.png" , "alt" : "Thunderbird" } ) ;
} ) ;
```

3. Now, add a statement in the script block to display the new alternative image text
```
$( "#out" ).text( img.attr( "alt" ) ) ;
```

4. Save the document alongside the jQuery library file then open it in a browser to see the manipulated attributes

Don't forget

Attribute values are always strings – with the exception of the **value** and **tabindex** attributes.

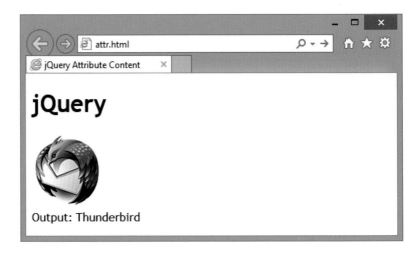

An attribute within an element in a jQuery object can be removed from the DOM simply by specifying its name as an argument to that object's **removeAttr()** method. There are subtle differences between attribute property values and state of the Boolean **checked**, **selected**, and **disabled** attributes – it is recommended that the **prop()** method be used to get or set these attributes:

1 Add a form with two checked boxes and a paragraph with two spans to the body of an HTML document
```
<form> <input id = "box1" type="checkbox" checked >
<input id = "box2" type="checkbox" checked > </form>
<p>Box1 Checked? : <span id = "out1" ></span>
<br>Box2 Checked? : <span id = "out2" ></span></p>
```

removeattr.html

2 In the head section of the HTML document add a script block that removes the checked attribute of the first box
```
$( document ).ready( function() {
  var b1 = $( "#box1" ) , b2 = $( "#box2" ) ;
  b1.removeAttr( "checked" ) ;
} ) ;
```

3 Now, add a statement in the script block to display the checked property value and attribute state of each box
```
$( "#out1" ).text( b1.prop( "checked" )
        + " | " + b1.attr( "checked" ) ) ;
$( "#out2" ).text( b2.prop( "checked" )
        + " | " + b2.attr( "checked" ) ) ;
```

4 Save the document alongside the jQuery library file then open it in a browser to see the attribute values and states

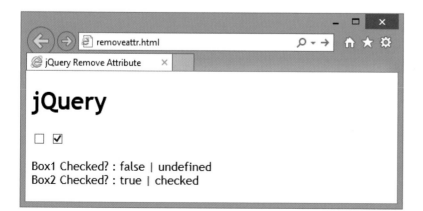

65

Hot tip

The HTML **checked** attribute actually corresponds to the **defaultChecked** property.

Adding content

Content can be added outside an element in a jQuery object by specifying it as an argument to that object's **before()** method, for addition immediately before the element, and to that object's **after()** method – for addition immediately after the element. Similarly, content can be inserted inside an element by specifying it as an argument to that object's **prepend()** and **append()** methods, for insertion at the beginning and end of the element:

prepend.html

1　Add a list to the body of an HTML document
```
<ul><li>Apple<li>Banana<li>Cherry</ul>
```

2　In the head section of the HTML document add a script block that adds content before and after the list
```
$(document).ready( function() {
  var list = $( "ul" ) ;
  list.before( "+ BEFORE" ) ;
  list.after( "+ AFTER" ) ;
} ) ;
```

3　Now, add statements in the script block to insert content inside the list at its beginning and end
```
list.prepend( "< PREPEND" ) ;
list.append( "< APPEND" ) ;
```

4　Save the document alongside the jQuery library file then open it in a browser to see the added content

Don't forget

The **before()** and **after()** methods add content outside the selected element whereas **prepend()** and **append()** methods add content inside the element.

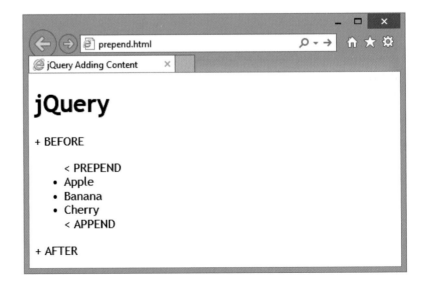

Content can also be added outside an element in a jQuery object using that object's **insertBefore()** and **insertAfter()** methods, or inserted inside an element using its **prependTo()** and **appendTo()** methods. Unlike the methods described opposite, these methods must be preceded by a content selector or markup string and take the target element as their argument:

1. Add a list to the body of an HTML document
`<ul><li>Apple<li>Banana<li>Cherry</ul>`

2. In the head section of the HTML document add a script block that adds content before and after the list
```
$(document).ready( function() {
  var list = $( "ul" ) ;
  $( "<p>+ BEFORE</p>" ).insertBefore( list ) ;
  $( "<p>+ AFTER</p>" ).insertAfter( list ) ;
} ) ;
```

3. Now, add statements in the script block to insert markup content inside the list at its beginning and end
```
$( "<span>< PREPEND</span>" ).prependTo( list ) ;
$( "<span>< APPEND</span>" ).appendTo( list ) ;
```

4. Save the document alongside the jQuery library file then open it in a browser to see the added content

prependto.html

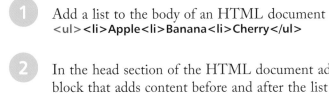

Beware

Markup content to be added to elements should include HTML tags, rather than be just text strings.

67

Wrapping elements

A containing element or HTML structure can be wrapped around an element in a jQuery object by specifying it as an argument to that object's **wrap()** method. Conversely, a containing element can be removed from around an element by specifying it as an argument to that object's **unwrap()** method:

wrap.html

1 Add ordered lists to the body of an HTML document
```
<ol id = "abc" ><li>Alpha<li>Bravo<li>Charlie</ol>
<ol id = "xyz" ><li>Xray<li>Yankee<li>Zulu</ol>
```

2 In the head section of the HTML document add a style sheet to specify rules for division elements
```
<style>
div { background:yellow; border:3px solid red; width:300px; }
</style>
```

3 Next, in the head section of the HTML document add a script block that first wraps a division around both lists, then unwraps the division around the first list
```
$(document).ready( function() {
  $( "#abc , #xyz" ).wrap( "<div></div>" ) ;
  $( "#abc" ).unwrap( "<div></div>" ) ;
} ) ;
```

4 Save the document alongside the jQuery library file then open it in a browser to see the wrapped element

Don't forget

The structure argument passed for wrapping should be correctly formed HTML – including closing tags.

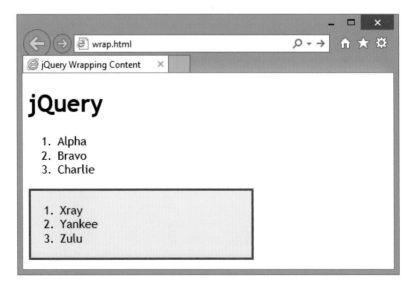

A containing element can be wrapped around an entire collection of elements in a jQuery object by specifying it as an argument to that object's **wrapAll()** method. Similarly a containing element can be wrapped around each individual element in a collection by specifying it as an argument to the object's **wrapInner()** method:

1. Add ordered lists to the body of an HTML document
```
<ol id = "abc" ><li>Alpha<li>Bravo<li>Charlie</ol>
<ol id = "xyz" ><li>Xray<li>Yankee<li>Zulu</ol>
```

wrapinner.html

2. In the head section of the HTML document add a style sheet to specify rules for division elements
```
<style>
div { background:yellow; border:3px solid red; width:300px; }
</style>
```

3. Next, in the head section of the HTML document, add a script block that first wraps all list items in the first list, then wraps each individual list item in the second list
```
$(document).ready( function() {
  $( "#abc li" ).wrapAll( "<div></div>" ) ;
  $( "#xyz li" ).wrapInner( "<div></div>" ) ;
} ) ;
```

4. Save the document alongside the jQuery library file then open it in a browser to see the wrapped elements

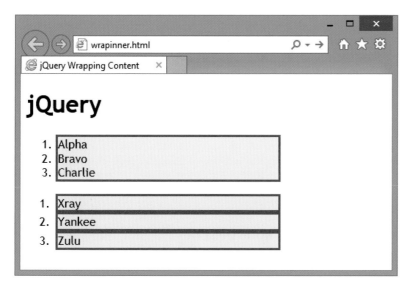

69

Hot tip

Elements to be wrapped may contain several nested levels – the wrapped element will contain the specified element and all its nested levels.

Replacing elements

An element or collection of elements in a jQuery object can be replaced by another element and content specified as an argument to that object's **replaceWith()** method.

Alternatively, replacement content can be specified before a jQuery object's **replaceAll()** method and the element to be replaced specified as that method's argument:

replace.html

1. Add an unordered list and a paragraph containing a span to the body of an HTML document
   ```
   <ul><li>ONE<li>TWO<li>THREE</ul>
   <p>Output: <span id = "out" ></span></p>
   ```

2. In the head section of the HTML document add a script block that displays each list item element tag and text
   ```
   $(document).ready( function() {
     var list = $( "ul" ) ;
     $( "#out" ).text( list.html() ) ;
   } ) ;
   ```

3. Next, in the script block, add statements to replace the unordered list elements with ordered list elements, then replace each list item element and their content
   ```
   list.replaceWith( "<ol>" + list.html() + "</ol>" ) ;
   $( "<li>List Item</li>" ).replaceAll( $( "li" ) ) ;
   ```

4. Save the document alongside the jQuery library file then open it in a browser to see the replaced elements

Don't forget

The **replaceAll()** method achieves similar results to the **replaceWith()** method but the syntax of its source and target is reversed.

70

An element contained in a jQuery object, together with all its child elements and contents, can be copied (cloned) using that object's **clone()** method. The copy can then, usefully, be inserted wherever required in the document. Content contained in the original element can be replaced simply by specifying new content as arguments to its **text()** or **html()** methods:

1. Add a regular numerically ordered list to the body of an HTML document
```
<ol><li>ONE<li>TWO<li>THREE</ol>
```

HTML

clone.html

2. In the head section of the HTML document add a script block that inserts a copy of the list into the document, after the original first list
```
$(document).ready( function() {
  var list = $( "ol" ) ;
  list.clone().insertAfter( list ) ;
} ) ;
```

Beware

Avoid cloning elements that have an ID attribute as they must be unique.

3. Next, in the script block, insert statements to replace the numbering style and contents of the original first list
```
list.css( "list-style-type" , "upper-alpha" ) ;
list.html( "<li>Alpha<li>Bravo<li>Charlie" ) ;
```

4. Save the document alongside the jQuery library file then open it in a browser to see the copied and replaced lists

Beware

User data typed into form input fields and dropdown list selections are not copied to cloned elements – these are set to their default values specified in the HTML.

71

Removing elements

All child elements and content of an element contained in a jQuery object can be removed using that object's **empty()** method. This retains the object element itself but that too can be removed, along with child elements and content, by the **remove()** method:

1 Add a division containing a paragraph with an inner span, followed by a paragraph containing two spans, to the body of an HTML document
```
<div id = "box" >Division Text
<p id="txt">Paragraph Text<span>Span Text</span></p>
</div>
<p>Paragraph Emptied: <span id = "out1" ></span>
<br>Paragraph Removed: <span id="out2"></span></p>
```

2 In the head section of the HTML document add a script block that empties the paragraph and display its parent's remaining contents
```
$(document).ready( function() {
  var parent = $( "#box" ) , child = $( "#txt" ) ;
  child.empty() ;
  $( "#out1" ).text( parent.html() ) ;
} ) ;
```

3 Next, in the script, block insert statements to remove the paragraph and display its parent's now remaining contents
```
  child.remove() ;
  $( "#out2" ).text( parent.html() ) ;
```

4 Save the document alongside the jQuery library file then open it in a browser to see the element emptied and removed

Don't forget

The **remove()** method removes an element and all its contents, whereas the **empty()** method merely removes an element's contents.

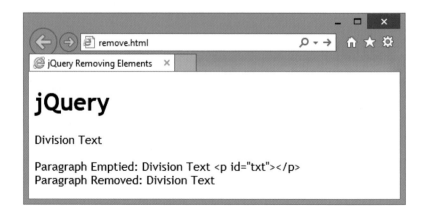

jQuery Removing Elements

jQuery

Division Text

Paragraph Emptied: Division Text <p id="txt"></p>
Paragraph Removed: Division Text

An element contained in a jQuery object that has been removed from the DOM using that object's **remove()** method loses any behaviors created by jQuery. Conversely, an element can be removed from the DOM and retain behaviors created by jQuery using that object's **detach()** method:

① Add a form containing two text input fields to the body of an HTML document
```
<form><input type="text" value = "Removed" >
<input type="text" value = "Detached" ></form>
```

detach.html

② In the head section of the HTML document add a script block that creates behaviors to change the background color of each input whenever it receives and loses focus
```
$(document).ready( function() {
  var fields = $( "input[type='text']" ) ;
  fields.focus( function() {
        $( this ).css( "background" , "red" ) ; } ) ;
  fields.blur( function() {
        $( this ).css( "background" , "white" ) ; } ) ;
} ) ;
```

③ Next, in the script block, insert statements to remove and append the first text input then detach and append the second text input – re-attaching both inputs to the form
```
fields.eq(0).remove().appendTo( "form" ) ;
fields.eq(1).detach().appendTo( "form" ) ;
```

④ Save the document alongside the jQuery library file then open it in a browser to see the second input retain behaviors

Hot tip

The **detach()** method is the same as the **remove()** method but as it keeps all jQuery data associated with the removed elements, it is more useful to re-attach elements to the DOM.

73

Attaching data

Data can be attached to an element contained in a jQuery object by specifying a key and associated value as a comma-separated pair of key:value arguments to that object's **data()** method. Attached values can be retrieved at any time by calling the object's **data()** method with their associated key as the argument:

data.html

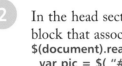 Add an image and a paragraph containing a span to the body of an HTML document
```
<img id ="pic" src = "roadster.png" >
<p>Output: <span id = "out" ></span></p>
```

2 In the head section of the HTML document add a script block that associates two key:value pairs with the image
```
$(document).ready( function() {
  var pic = $( "#pic" ) ;
  pic.data( "Make" , "Jaguar" ) ;
  pic.data( "Model" , " F-Type" ) ;
} ) ;
```

3 Next, in the script block, insert a statement to display both data values associated with the image
```
$( "#out" ).text( pic.data( "Make" ) + pic.data( "Model" ) ) ;
```

4 Save the document alongside the jQuery library file then open it in a browser to see the data associated with the element

Beware

The **data()** method cannot be used on **<object>** (unless it's a Flash plugin), **<applet>** or **<embed>** elements.

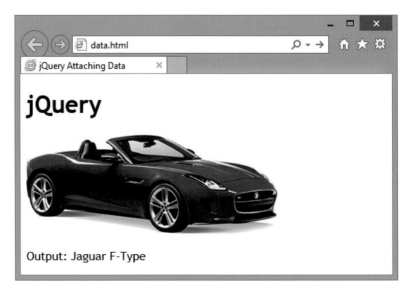

Data that has been attached to an element contained in a jQuery object using its **data()** method can be removed by specifying the value's associated key as an argument to its **removeData()** method. Attempting to retrieve removed data will then return "undefined":

1 Add an image and a paragraph containing a span to the body of an HTML document
```
<img id = "pic" src = "coupe.png" >
<p>Output: <span id = "out" ></span></p>
```

removedata.html

2 In the head section of the HTML document add a script block that associates two key:value pairs with the image
```
$(document).ready( function() {
  var pic = $( "#pic" ) ;
  pic.data( "Make" , "Porsche " ) ;
  pic.data( "Model" , "Cayman" ) ;
} ) ;
```

3 Next, in the script block insert statements to remove one value then try to display both associated data values
```
  pic.removeData( "Model" ) ;
  $( "#out" ).text( pic.data( "Make" ) + pic.data( "Model" ) ) ;
```

4 Save the document alongside the jQuery library file then open it in a browser to see the data associated with the element

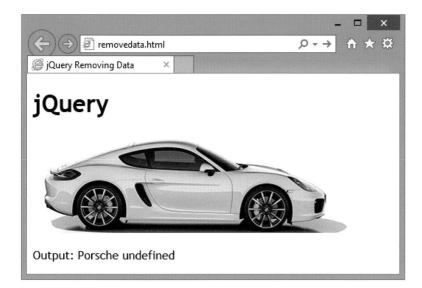

Hot tip

Associated data values can also be 'removed' by setting them to **null**. For example, by calling here **pic.data("Model", null)**.

Storing data

The intrinsic jQuery **$.hasData()** method can be used to determine whether a particular HTML element has attached data by specifying the element as its argument. The **$.hasData()** method returns **true** only when attached data is found. The element can be specified by referencing the first array item of a jQuery object:

hasdata.html

1. Add an image and a paragraph containing a span to the body of an HTML document
```
<img id = "pic" src = "classic.png" >
<p>Output: <span id = "out" ></span></p>
```

2. In the head section of the HTML document add a script block that associates data with the image
```
$(document).ready( function() {
  var pic = $( "#pic" ).data( "fg" , "red" ) ;
} ) ;
```

3. Next, in the script block, insert statements to display content only if data is associated with the image element
```
if( $.hasData( pic[0] ) ) {
$( "#out" ).text( pic[0] +
        " Has Data" ).css( "color" , pic.data( "fg" ) ) ; }
```

4. Save the document alongside the jQuery library file then open it in a browser to see content if data is associated

76

Multiple data items can be attached to an HTML element in a single statement by creating a JavaScript object of comma-separated key:value pairs enclosed within **{ }** braces. As usual, each value can then be referenced using its associated key:

1. Add an image and a paragraph containing a span to the body of an HTML document
```
<img id = "pic" src = "drophead.png" >
<p>Output: <span id = "out" ></span></p>
```

dataobject.html

2. In the head section of the HTML document add a script block that associates key:value pairs with the image
```
$(document).ready( function() {
  var pic = $( "#pic" ) ;
  pic.data( "info" , { make: "Lamborghini " ,
            model: "Gallardo " , version: "Spyder" } ) ;
} ) ;
```

3. Next, in the script block, insert statements to display all associated data values
```
$( "#out" ).text( pic.data( "info" ).make +
pic.data( "info" ).model + pic.data( "info" ).version ) ;
```

Hot tip

Data is retained for elements that have been removed using the **detach()** method if they are re-attached later.

4. Save the document alongside the jQuery library file then open it in a browser to see the data associated with the element

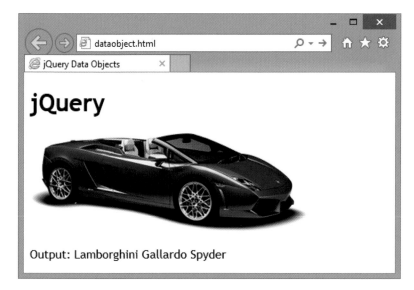

Output: Lamborghini Gallardo Spyder

Hot tip

Calling the **data()** method with no arguments retrieves all the values as a JavaScript object that can be assigned to a variable.

Summary

- An element's text content can be retrieved or added using the jQuery object's **text()** method

- An element's text and HTML tag content can both be retrieved or added using the jQuery object's **html()** method

- An element's attribute value can be retrieved or added using the jQuery object's **attr()** method

- An element's attribute can be removed from the DOM using the jQuery object's **removeAttr()** method

- Content can be added <u>outside</u> an element using the **before()**, **insertBefore()**, **after()** and **insertAfter()** methods

- Content can be added <u>inside</u> an element using the **prepend()**, **prependTo()**, **append()** and **appendTo()** methods

- An HTML structure can be added around an element using the **wrap()** method or removed using the **unwrap()** method

- An HTML structure can be added around a collection of elements using the **wrapAll()** and **wrapInner()** methods

- An element or collection of elements can be replaced using the **replaceWith()** and **replaceAll()** methods

- An element's content and descendants can be copied using the **clone()** method or removed using the **empty()** method

- An element can be removed together with its content and descendants using the **remove()** or **detach()** methods

- Only elements removed using the **detach()** method retain data and behaviors created by jQuery when re-attached later

- Data can be attached as argument pairs to the **data()** method and its existence confirmed using the **hasData()** method

- Data attached to an element can be retrieved using the **data()** method and removed using the **removeData()** method

5 Recognizing events

This chapter demonstrates how to create event-handler functions that provide responses to user actions.

Detecting clicks

When the user clicks, or taps, on an element in a jQuery object a "click event" occurs that can be recognized by that object's **click()** method. Similarly, when the user makes a double-click on the element a "dblclick event" occurs that can be recognized by that object's **dblclick()** method. An anonymous function argument can be specified to each method to provide a response to each event:

click.html

1 Add a division to the body of an HTML document
`<div id = "box" >`**Click Box**`</div>`

2 In the head section of the HTML document add a style sheet to specify initial rules for the division
```
<style>
#box { border:2px dashed gray; width:200px; height:50px; }
</style>
```

3 Next, in the head section of the document, add a script block that specifies event-handlers for each click event
```
$( document ).ready( function() {

    var box = $( "#box" ).click( function() {
            $( this ).css ( "background" , "yellow" ) ;
            $( this ).text( "Click Detected" ) ;          } ) ;

    box.dblclick( function() {
            $( this ).css ( "background" , "aqua" ) ;
            $( this ).text( "Double-Click Detected" ) ; } ) ;
} ) ;
```

4 Save the document alongside the jQuery library file then open it in a browser and click the division to see response

Don't forget

The **css()** and **text()** methods could be chained together here in a single statement with `$( this ).css(...).text(...);`.

80

The "click event" of an element in a jQuery object can be fired from the script by calling that object's **trigger()** method and specifying the event name (within quote marks) as its argument. This will execute the statements within that event's nominated event-handler function as if the user had clicked on the element:

1 Add a division to the body of an HTML document
```
<div id = "box" >Click Box</div>
```

triggerclick.html

2 In the head section of the HTML document add a style sheet to specify initial rules for the division
```
<style>
#box { border:2px dashed gray; width:300px; height:50px; }
</style>
```

3 Next, in the head section of the document, add a script block that specifies a click event-handler for the division
```
$( document ).ready( function() {

    var box = $( "#box" ).click( function() {
            $( this ).css ( "background" , "lime" ). ;
            $( this ).text( "Click Triggered" ) ;          } ) ;
} ) ;
```

4 Now, in the script block, add a statement to trigger the division's click event and call its event-handler function
```
box.trigger( "click" ) ;
```

5 Save the document alongside the jQuery library file then open it in a browser to see the triggered click event

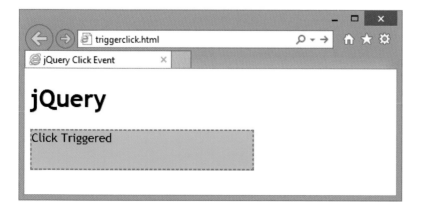

Hot tip

Notice how these event-handler functions efficiently reference the element with **$(this)**.

Feeling pressure

When the user presses a mouse button down while the cursor is over an element in a jQuery object a "mousedown event" occurs that can be recognized by that object's **mousedown()** method. Similarly, when the user releases the mouse button while over the element a "mouseup event" occurs that can be recognized by that object's **mouseup()** method. An anonymous function argument can be specified to each method to provide a response to each event:

mousebutton.html

1 Add a division to the body of an HTML document
`<div id = "box" >`**Click Box**`</div>`

2 In the head section of the HTML document add a style sheet to specify initial rules for the division
```
<style>
#box { border:2px dashed gray; width:200px; height:50px; }
</style>
```

3 Next, in the head section of the document, add a script block that sets event-handlers for mouse button events
```
$( document ).ready( function() {

  var box = $( "#box" ).mousedown( function() {
        $( this ).css ( "background" , "yellow" ) ;
        $( this ).text( "Mouse Button Pressed" ) ; } ) ;
  box.mouseup( function() {
        $( this ).css ( "background" , "aqua" ) ;
        $( this ).text( "Mouse Button Released" ) ; } ) ;
} ) ;
```

4 Save the document alongside the jQuery library file then open it in a browser and click the division to see response

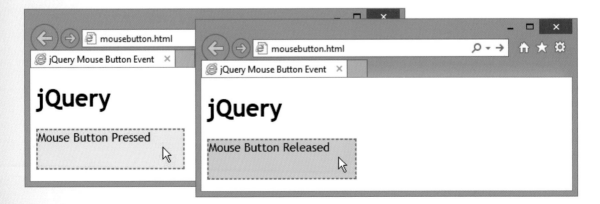

The mouse button events of an element in a jQuery object can be fired from the script by calling that object's **trigger()** method and specifying the event name (within quote marks) as its argument. This will execute the statements within that event's nominated event-handler function as if the user had clicked on the element:

1 Add a division to the body of an HTML document
`<div id = "box" >Click Box</div>`

2 In the head section of the HTML document add a style sheet to specify initial rules for the division
```
<style>
#box { border:2px dashed gray; width:300px; height:50px; }
</style>
```

3 Next, in the head section of the document, add a script block that sets a mousedown event-handler for the division
```
$( document ).ready( function() {

  var box = $( "#box" ).mousedown( function() {
    $( this ).css ( "background" , "lime" ) ;
    $( this ).text( "Mouse Button Down Triggered" ) ; } ) ;
} ) ;
```

4 Now, in the script block, add a statement to trigger the division's mousedown event and call its event-handler
`box.trigger( "mousedown" ) ;`

5 Save the document alongside the jQuery library file then open it in a browser to see the triggered mousedown event

triggermousedown.html

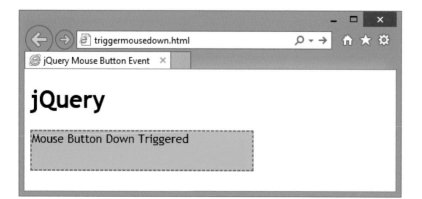

Hot tip

Mutiple event-handlers can be chained together into a single lengthy statement – but are more easily readable as separate statements.

Detecting presence

When the user moves the mouse cursor over an element in a jQuery object a "mouseover event" occurs that can be recognized by that object's **mouseover()** method. Similarly, when the user moves the mouse cursor out of the element's box area a "mouseout event" occurs that can be recognized by that object's **mouseout()** method. An anonymous function argument can be specified to each method to provide a response to each event:

mouseover.html

1 Add a division to the body of an HTML document
```
<div id= "zone" >Mouse Zone</div>
```

2 In the head section of the HTML document add a style sheet to specify initial rules for the division
```
<style>
#zone { border:2px dashed gray; width:200px; height:50px; }
</style>
```

3 Next, in the head section of the document, add a script block that sets event-handlers for mouse events
```
$( document ).ready( function() {

  var zone = $( "#zone" ).mouseover( function() {
    $( this ).text( "Over" ).css( "background" ,"yellow" ) ; } ) ;

zone.mouseout( function() {
    $( this ).text( "Out" ).css( "background" ,"aqua" ) ; } ) ;
} ) ;
```

4 Save the document alongside the jQuery library file then open it in a browser and move the cursor to see detection

Beware

Mouseover events bubble down to inner elements – so their event-handler may also be triggered when the cursor is over a contained inner element.

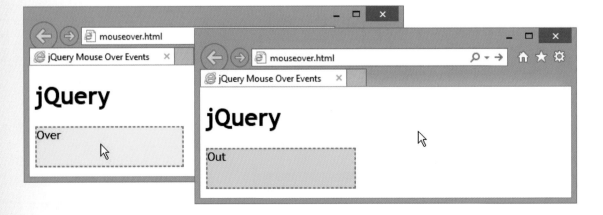

Optionally, a jQuery event recognition method can specify an additional argument when nominating an event-handler to pass a value to the handler function. Multiple values can also be specified as key:value pairs in a JavaScript object argument and the event passed to the event-handler function. Those values can then be referenced using their key with the event object's **data** property:

1. Add a division to the body of an HTML document
```
<div id = "zone" >Mouse Zone</div>
```

HTML

eventdata.html

2. In the head section of the HTML document add a style sheet to specify initial rules for the division
```
<style>
#zone { border:2px dashed gray; width:200px; height:50px; }
</style>
```

3. Next, in the head section of the document, add a script block that sets mouse event-handlers for the division
```
$( document ).ready( function() {

  var zone = $( "#zone" ).mouseover( on="Mouse Over" ,
    function() {
      $( this ).text( on ).css( "background" , "lime" ) ; } ) ;

  zone.mouseout( { off:"Mouse Out", hue:"fuchsia" } ,
    function(e) { $( this ).text( e.data.off ) ;
      $( this ).css( "background" , e.data.hue ) ; } ) ;
} ) ;
```

Hot tip

It is commonplace to use the letter **e** to represent the event when passing it to the event-handler function as an argument.

4. Save the document alongside the jQuery library file then open it in a browser and move the cursor to see detection

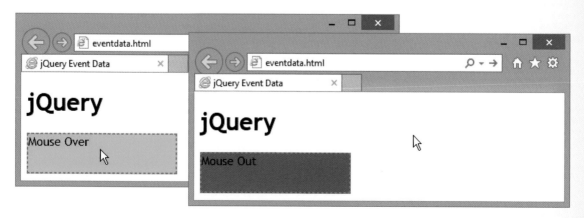

Guarding borders

When the user moves the mouse cursor onto an element in a jQuery object a "mouseenter event" occurs that can be recognized by that object's **mouseenter()** method. Similarly, when the user moves the mouse cursor off the element's box area a "mouseleave event" occurs that can be recognized by that object's **mouseleave()** method. An anonymous function argument can be specified to each method to provide a response to each event:

mouseenter.html

Don't forget

The mouseover or mouseenter events are triggered when the cursor enters the element's border area.

1) Add a division to the body of an HTML document
`<div id = "zone" >Mouse Zone</div>`

2) In the head section of the HTML document add a style sheet to specify initial rules for the division
```
<style>
#zone { border:2px dashed gray; width:200px; height:50px; }
</style>
```

3) Next, in the head section of the document, add a script block that sets event-handlers for mouse events
```
$( document ).ready( function() {

  var zone = $( "#zone" ).mouseenter( function() {
    $( this ).text( "Enter" ).css( "background" ,"yellow" ) ; } ) ;

zone.mouseleave( function() {
    $( this ).text( "Leave" ).css( "background","aqua" ) ; } ) ;
} ) ;
```

4) Save the document alongside the jQuery library file then open it in a browser and move the cursor to see response

Unlike the "mouseover" and "mouseout" events the "mouseenter" and "mouseleave" events do not bubble across the DOM – so are not triggered by mouse actions on inner nested elements:

1 Add two divisions that each contain a paragraph to the body of an HTML document
```
<div id = "d1" ><p id = "p1" >0 Entries</p></div>
<div id = "d2" ><p id = "p2" >0 Overs</p></div>
```

eventbubble.html

2 In the head section of the HTML document add a style sheet to specify rules for the divisions and paragraphs
```
<style>
div { background:aqua; width:100px; float:left; margin:10px }
p { background: yellow; margin: 10px; }
</style>
```

3 Next, in the head section of the document, add a script block that sets event-handlers for mouse events
```
$( document ).ready( function() {

    var en = 0 , ov = 0 ; // Counter variables.
    $( "#d1" ).mouseenter( function() {
         $( "#p1" ).text( ++en + " Entries" ) ; } ) ;
    $( "#d2" ).mouseover( function() {
         $( "#p2" ).text( ++ov + " Overs" ) ; } ) ;
} ) ;
```

Hot tip

Use the **mouseenter()** and **mouseleave()** methods rather than **mouseover()** and **mouseout()** to avoid event bubbling problems.

4 Save the document alongside the jQuery library file then open it in a browser and move the cursor onto each paragraph once – to see that only the "mouseover" event fires on both outer division and inner paragraph elements

Spotting movement

When the user moves the mouse cursor over an element in a jQuery object a "mousemove event" occurs that can be recognized by that object's **mousemove()** method. An anonymous function can be specified to this method as an event-handler and the event object can be passed to this as an argument. The event has **pageX** and **pageY** properties that contain the current cursor coordinates as pixel values relative to the top left corner of the document:

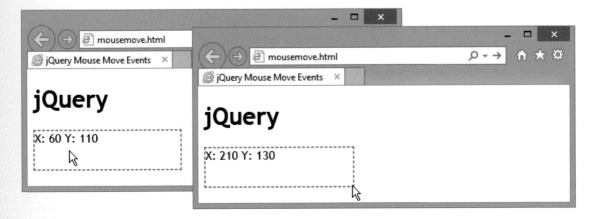

mousemove.html

1 Add a division to the body of an HTML document
`<div id = "zone" >Mouse Zone</div>`

2 In the head section of the HTML document add a style sheet to specify initial rules for the division
`<style>`
`#zone { border:2px dashed gray; width:200px; height:50px; }`
`</style>`

3 Next, in the head section of the document, add a script block that sets an event-handler for mouse movement that displays the cursor position within the document
```
$( document ).ready( function() {

  $( "#zone" ).mousemove( function( e ) {
    var left = e.pageX ;
    var top = e.pageY ;
    $( this ).text( "X: " + left + " Y: " + top ) ; } ) ;
} ) ;
```

4 Save the document alongside the jQuery library file then open it in a browser and move the cursor to see position

Don't forget

The coordinates stored in the mousemove event pageX and pageY properties are relative to the document edges – not the element edges.

---

mousemove.html
jQuery Mouse Move Events ✕

jQuery

X: 60 Y: 110

mousemove.html
jQuery Mouse Move Events ✕

jQuery

X: 210 Y: 130

When tracking the mouse cursor it is often desirable to reference its coordinates within the element rather than those within the document. This is simply achieved by subtracting the element's **offsetLeft** and **offsetTop** property values from the coordinates:

1. Add a division to the body of an HTML document
```
<div id = "zone" >Mouse Zone</div>
```

2. In the head section of the HTML document add a style sheet to specify initial rules for the division
```
<style>
#zone { border:2px dashed gray; width:200px; height:50px; }
</style>
```

3. Next, in the head section of the document, add a script block that displays the cursor position within the element
```
$( document ).ready( function() {
  $( "#zone" ).mousemove( function( e ) {
  var left = ( e.pageX - this.offsetLeft ) ;
  var top = ( e.pageY - this.offsetTop ) ;
  $( this ).text( "X: " + left + " Y: " + top ) ; } ) ;
} ) ;
```

4. Now, in the script block, add a statement to apply a background style appropriate to the cursor's position
```
if ( left < 100 ) $( this ).css( "background" , "yellow" ) ;
else $( this ).css( "background" , "aqua" ) ;
```

5. Save the document alongside the jQuery library file then open it in a browser and move the cursor to see position

mousetrack.html

Hot tip

You can use this technique to reference coordinates relative to the top left corner of the element in any browser.

89

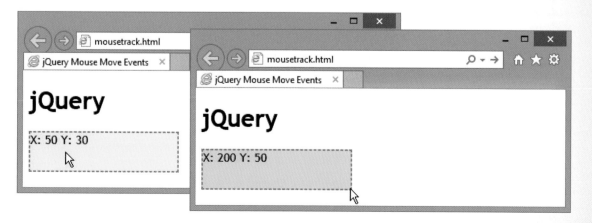

Detecting keys

When the user presses a keyboard key on an in-focus element of a jQuery object, a "keypress event" occurs that can be recognized by that object's **keypress()** method. An anonymous function can be specified to this method as an event-handler and the event object can be passed to this as an argument. The event has a **which** property that contains the Character Code number of the key pressed – alphabet keys are 65-90 for a-z and 97-122 for A-Z:

keypress.html

1. Add a form text input and a paragraph containing a span to the body of an HTML document
```
<form><input type="text" id = "txt" maxlength="1">
</form> <p>Output: <span id = "out" ></span></p>
```

Don't forget

The keypress event recognizes the ASCII Character Code number of the key pressed.

2. In the head section of the HTML document add a script block that sets a keypress handler to clear the text input
```
$( document ).ready( function() {
  $( "#txt" ).keypress( function( e ) {
    $( this ).val( null ) ;                         } ) ;
} ) ;
```

Beware

Characters Codes and Key Codes are subtly different – the Character Code is 65 for character "A" and 97 for character "a" but the Key Code for the 'A' key is always 65.

3. Next, in the event-handler, insert statements to identify the character code and to display the character type
```
var str = "Non-Alpha" ;
if ( (e.which > 64)  && (e.which < 91) ) str = "Uppercase" ;
else
if ( (e.which > 96)  && (e.which < 123) ) str = "Lowercase" ;
$( "#out" ).text(  str + " Character Pressed" ) ;
```

4. Save the document alongside the jQuery library file then open it in a browser and type any character in the input

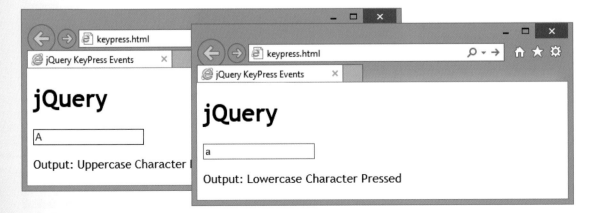

90

A "keydown event" occurs when the user holds down a keyboard key and can be recognized by that object's **keydown()** method. Similarly, a "keyup event" occurs when the user releases a keyboard key and can be recognized by that object's **keyup()** method. The event passed as an argument to their event-handlers has a **which** property that contains the Key Code number of the key pressed:

1. Add a form text input and a paragraph containing a span to the body of an HTML document
```
<form><input type="text" id = "txt" maxlength="1">
</form> <p>Output: <span id = "out" ></span></p>
```

2. In the head section of the HTML document add a script block that sets a keydown handler to display Key Code
```
$( document ).ready( function() {

  var txt = $( "#txt" ) , out = $( "#out" ) ;
  txt.keydown( function( e ) {
    out.text( "Key " + e.which + " Down" ) ; } ) ;
} ) ;
```

3. Next, in the script block, insert a keyup handler to clear the text input and display a release confirmation
```
txt.keyup( function( e ) {
        $( this ).val( null ) ;
        out.text( "Key " + e.which + " Up" ) ;
} ) ;
```

4. Save the document alongside the jQuery library file then open it in a browser and type any character in the input

keydown.html

Don't forget

The keydown event recognizes the Key Code number that identifies the key pressed irrespective of case.

Hot tip

Use keydown to detect special keys by code number – such as the arrow keys (37-40).

91

jQuery

? ✕

Output: Key 191 Down

jQuery

Output: Key 191 Up

Adjusting size

When the user resizes the browser window, a "resize event" occurs that is sent to the DOM **window** object and this event can be recognized by that object's **resize()** method. An anonymous function can be specified to this method as an event-handler to provide a response when the window size gets adjusted.

Implementation of the resize event varies between browsers, with some firing only after completion of the resize and others firing both at the start and end of the resizing action. A timer can usefully be employed to ensure the resize event-handler is only called once in any browser – after completion of the resize:

resize.html

1 Add a division and a paragraph containing a span to the body of an HTML document
```
<div>Resize the browser window.</div>
<p>Output: <span id = "out" ></span></p>
```

2 In the head section of the HTML document add a script block that initializes counter and timer variables
```
$( document ).ready( function() {
  var num = 0 , timer = null ;
} ) ;
```

3 Next, in the script block, insert a function to set the background color of the division and display window size
```
function showsize() {

  num++ ;
  var hue = ( num % 2 === 0 ) ? "yellow" : "aqua" ;
  $( "div" ).css( "background" , hue ) ;

  var str = num + " - Browser" ;
  str += " Width: " + $( window ).width() ;
  str += " Height: "+ $( window ).height() ;
  $( "#out" ).text( str ) ;
}
```

Don't forget

This example alternates the background color of the division according to the parity (odd or even) value of the counter.

4 Now, in the script block, add a resize event-handler that calls the function once to confirm resize has completed
```
$( window ).resize(function () {

  clearTimeout( timer) ;
  timer = setTimeout( showsize , 100 ) ;
} ) ;
```

5 Save the document alongside the jQuery library file then open it in any browser and resize to see the responses

Beware

Code in a resize event-handler should never rely on the number of times the handler is called as resize events can be sent continuously as the resizing is in progress.

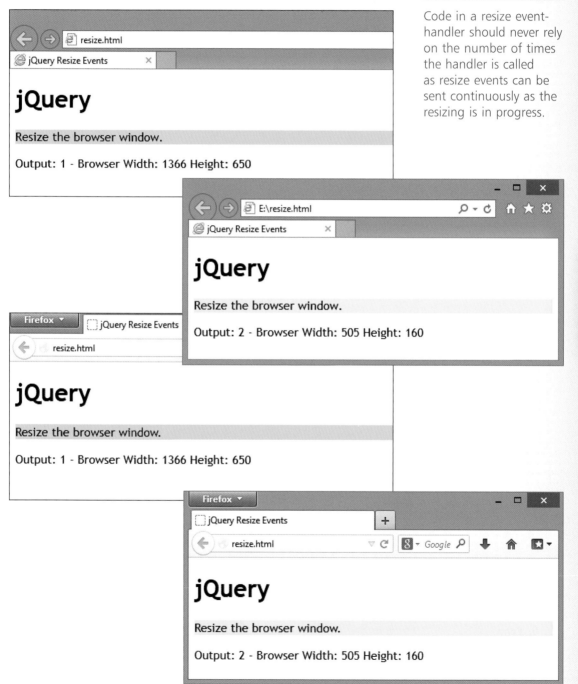

Scrolling around

When the user scrolls an element of a jQuery object, a "scroll event" occurs that can be recognized by that object's **scroll()** method. An anonymous function can be specified to this method as an event-handler to recognize that user action:

1 Add an ordered list and a paragraph containing a span to the body of an HTML document

```
<ol id = "list" ><li>Alpha<li>Bravo<li>Charlie
        <li>Delta<li>Echo<li>Foxtrot<li>Golf</ol>
<p>Output: <span id = "out" ></span></p>
```

scroll.html

2 In the head section of the HTML document add a style sheet to specify rules for the list that allow scrolling

```
<style> ol { border:1px solid gray ; ]
#list { overflow-y: scroll ; width: 150px ; height: 90px ; }
</style>
```

3 Next, in the head section of the HTML document, add a script block that sets a scroll handler to count scrolls

```
$( document ).ready( function() {
  var num = 0 ;
  $( "#list" ).scroll( function() {
    num++;
    $( "#out" ).text( "Scrolls Detected = " + num ) ; } ) ;
} ) ;
```

Hot tip

You can call the **scroll()** method of an element without an argument to scroll the element.

4 Save the document alongside the jQuery library file then open it in a browser and scroll the list to see the count

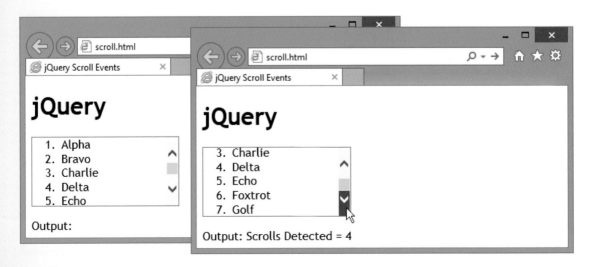

When scrolling an element of a jQuery object, its pixel offset along the X and Y axis from its original position can be revealed by calling its **scrollLeft()** and **scrollTop()** methods:

1 Add two nested divisions and a paragraph containing a span to the body of an HTML document
```
<div id = "box" ><div id = "txt" >Content</div></div>
<p>Offset: <span id = "out" >X: 0 Y: 0</span></p>
```

scrollaxis.html

2 In the head section of the HTML document add a style sheet to specify size and scroll rules for the divisions
```
<style>
div { width: 200px; height: 100px; border: 1px solid gray; }
#box { overflow: scroll ; }
#txt { margin: 50px ; background: yellow ; }
</style>
```

3 Next, in the head section of the HTML document, add a script block that displays scrolled offset values
```
$( document ).ready( function() {
  $( "#box" ).scroll( function() {
    var x = $( this ).scrollLeft() + " pixels" ;
    var y = $( this ).scrollTop()  + " pixels" ;
    $( "#out" ).text( "X: " + x + " Y: " + y ) ; } ) ;
} ) ;
```

Don't forget

The horizontal and vertical scroll positions are the same as the number of pixels that are hidden from view in the scrollable area.

4 Save the document alongside the jQuery library file then open it in a browser and scroll to see the offsets

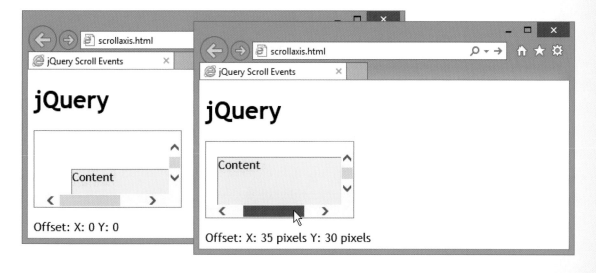

Summary

- Click events on an element in a jQuery object can be recognized by that object's **click()** and **dblclick()** methods

- An event-handler can be specified as an argument to those methods that recognize events to provide dynamic responses

- An event can be fired by specifying its name within quote marks as an argument to a jQuery object's **trigger()** method

- Mouse button events that occur while over an element can be recognized by the **mousedown()** and **mouseup()** methods

- Mouse movement events that occur over an element can be recognized by the **mouseover()**, **mouseout()**, **mouseenter()**, **mouseleave()**, and **mousemove()** methods

- An event can be passed to an event-handler as an argument and multiple values can be specified in a JavaScript object

- A value in a JavaScript object passed to an event-handler can be referenced by their associated key with the **data** property

- The mousemove object has **pageX** and **pageY** properties that contain cursor position relative to the top left of the document

- Key events of an element in a jQuery object can be recognized by that object's **keypress()**, **keydown()**, and **keyup()** methods

- Key events passed to the **keypress()** method have a **which** property that contains a Character Code numeric value

- Key events passed to the **keydown()** and **keyup()** methods have a **which** property that contains a Key Code numeric value

- Resize events are sent to the DOM **window** object and can be recognized by that object's **resize()** method

- Scroll events of an element in a jQuery object can be recognized by that object's **scroll()** method

- The offset position of a scrolled element in a jQuery object can be revealed by calling its **scrollLeft()** and **scrollTop()** methods

6 Attaching handlers

This chapter demonstrates how to attach event-handlers and callback functions to events.

Binding to an event

jQuery methods such as **click()**, **focus()**, **mouseenter()**, and **submit()**, which recognize browser events, usefully allow an event-handler to be specified to provide a response to like-named browser events.

Event-handlers can also be attached ("bound") to browser events by specifying the event name and handler as comma-separated arguments to the jQuery object's more versatile **on()** method – using this syntax: ***jQuery-object*.on(** *event-name* **,** *event-handler* **)**

Event names that can be used to bind handlers to browser events are listed in the table below, together with a brief description of when each event fires in the browser:

Hot tip

Methods that recognize browser events, such as the **click()** and **focus()** methods, are often referred to as "shortcut methods" – shortcuts to the **on()** method.

Event name:	Event fires when:
blur	A form \<input\> field loses focus
change	The value of a form field changes
click	An element gets clicked
dblclick	An element gets double-clicked
focus	A form \<input\> field gains focus
keypress	A keyboard key is pressed down
keydown	A keyboard key is going down
keyup	A keyboard key is going up
mousedown	The left mouse button is pressed down
mouseup	The left mouse button is released up
mouseover	The mouse pointer is over the element
mouseout	The mouse pointer leaves the element
mouseenter	The mouse pointer enters over the element
mouseleave	The mouse pointer exits from the element
mousemove	The mouse pointer moves within the element
resize	The browser window changes size
scroll	The user scrolls the element
select	Text gets selected in a text area or a text field
submit	A form gets submitted

Don't forget

The event name must be enclosed within quote marks as an argument to the **on()** method.

Binding an event-handler to a browser event with the **on()** method causes the statements within the specified handler function to be executed each time that event fires in the browser. Alternatively, an event name and handler can be specified as arguments to the jQuery **one()** method to bind an event-handler to a browser event that will execute its statements only once – on the very first occasion the specified event fires in the browser:

1. Add a button and a paragraph containing a span to the body of an HTML document
```
<button id = "btn" >Click Me</button>
<p>Output: <span id = "out" ></span></p>
```

bindhandler.html

2. In the head section of the HTML document add a script block that binds an event-handler to run only once
```
$( document ).ready( function() {
  $( "#btn" ).one( "mouseenter" , function() {
       $( "p" ).prepend( "Count " ) ;    }       ) ;
} ) ;
```

3. Next, in the script block, insert statements that bind an event-handler to run each time a browser event fires
```
var num = 0 ;
$( "#btn" ).on( "click" , function() {
  num++ ;
  $( "#out" ).text( num ) ;      }      ) ;
```

Hot tip

The **on()** method provides all functionality required for attaching event-handlers and replaces the **bind()**, **delegate()**, and **live()** methods found in older version of jQuery.

69

4. Save the document alongside the jQuery library file then open it in a browser and click the button to see response

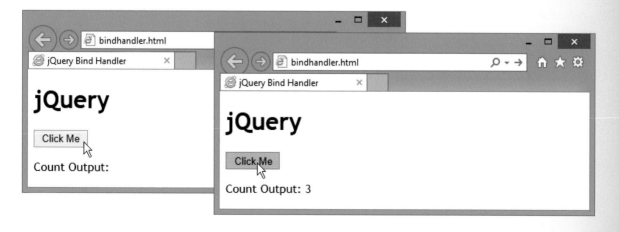

Binding multiple handlers

The versatility of the jQuery **on()** method allows multiple event-handlers to be specified as a JavaScript object argument that defines event names and associated handlers:

multihandler.html

1 Add a division and a paragraph containing a span to the body of an HTML document
```
<div id = "zone" >Click Zone</div>
<p>Output: <span id = "out" ></span></p>
```

2 In the head section of the HTML document add a style sheet to specify initial rules for the division
```
<style>
#zone { border:2px dashed gray; width:200px; height:50px; }
</style>
```

Don't forget

A reference to the span element in this example of **var out = $("#out")** could alternatively be used to avoid repetition.

3 Next, in the head section of the document, add a script block that recognizes browser events on the division
```
$( document ).ready( function() {
  $( "#zone" ).on(
  // Event-handlers statements to be inserted here.
  ) ;
} ) ;
```

4 Next, in the script block, insert statements that bind multiple event-handlers to events on the division
```
  {
    mouseenter: function() {
      $( this ).css( "background" , "yellow" ) ;
      $( "#out" ).text( "Mouse Entered" ) ;          }
    ,
    mousedown:  function() {
      $( this ).css( "background" , "lime" ) ;
      $( "#out" ).text( "Mouse Button Down" ) ;  }
    ,
    mouseup:    function() {
      $( this ).css( "background" , "fuchsia" ) ;
      $( "#out" ).text( "Mouse Button Up" ) ;        }
    ,
    mouseleave: function() {
      $( this ).css( "background" , "aqua" ) ;
      $( "#out" ).text( "Mouse Exited" ) ;           }
  }
```

Beware

Each event:handler pair specified in the JavaScript object must be separated by a comma character.

5 Save the document alongside the jQuery library file then open it in a browser and click the division to see response

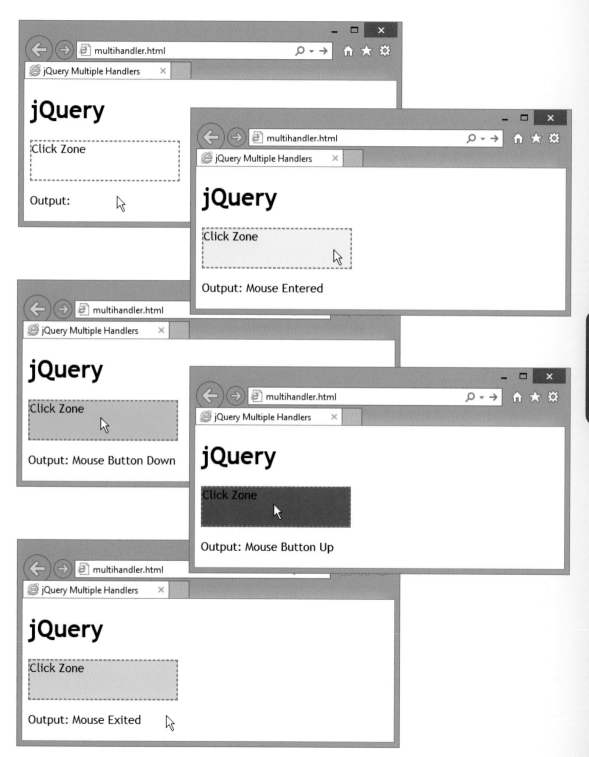

Passing event data

The jQuery **on()** method may, optionally, contain three arguments to specify an event name, data to be passed to the event-handler, and the handler function to be called when the named event fires. Multiple items of data can be stored within the event object in a JavaScript object of comma-separated key:value pairs. Passing the event object to the event-handler then enables each stored value to be referenced by its key in the event object's **data** property:

datahandler.html

1. Add a division and a paragraph containing a span to the body of an HTML document
```
<div id = "zone" >Click Zone</div>
<p>Output: <span id = "out" ></span></p>
```

2. In the head section of the HTML document add a style sheet to specify initial rules for the division
```
<style>
#zone { border:2px dashed gray; width:200px; height:50px; }
</style>
```

3. Next, in the head section of the document, add a script block that defines an event-handler to use passed data
```
$( document ).ready( function() {
  function handler( event ) {
    $( "#out" ).text( "Mouse " + event.data.msg ) ;
    $( this ).css( "background" , event.data.bg ) ;
  }
} ) ;
```

Hot tip

This example provides an alternative way to achieve the same effect as the previous example (which employs four functions) by passing data to a single function.

4. Next, in the script block, insert statements that recognize mouse events by passing data to the event-handler
```
$( "#zone" ).on( "mouseenter" ,
      { msg: "Entered" , bg: "yellow" } , handler ) ;

$( "#zone" ).on( "mousedown" ,
      { msg: "Button Down" , bg: "lime" } , handler ) ;

$( "#zone" ).on( "mouseup" ,
      { msg: "Button Up" , bg: "fuchsia" } , handler ) ;

$( "#zone" ).on( "mouseleave" ,
      { msg: "Exited" , bg: "aqua" } , handler ) ;
```

5. Save the document alongside the jQuery library file then open it in a browser and click the division to see response

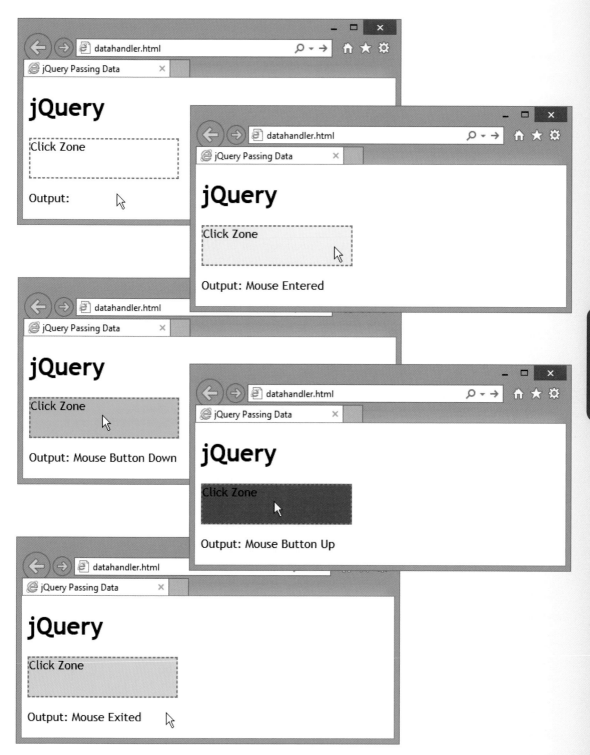

Triggering handlers

Once an event-handler has been defined for an element in a jQuery object it is executed whenever the event fires but can also be executed by remotely calling that element's **trigger()** method. This method simply requires the name of the event to which the handler is attached to be specified as its argument:

triggerhandler.html

1 Add a division plus paragraphs containing two buttons and a span to the body of an HTML document
```
<div id = "box" >Active Box</div>
<p>    <button id = "entr-btn" >Enter</button>
           <button id = "leave-btn" >Leave</button> </p>
<p>Output: <span id = "out" ></span></p>
```

2 In the head section of the HTML document add a style sheet to specify initial rules for the division
```
<style>
#box { border:2px dashed gray; width:200px; height:50px; }
</style>
```

Don't forget

A call to the **trigger()** method executes the event handler in just the same way as if the event had been fired normally by a user action.

3 Next, in the head section of the document, add a script block that defines an event-handler to use passed data
```
$( document ).ready( function() {
  function handler( event ) {
    $( "#out" ).text( event.data.action ) ;
    $( "#box" ).css( "background" , event.data.bg ) ;
  }
  // Trigger statements to be inserted here.
} ) ;
```

Hot tip

You can also specify a custom-named event to the **on()** method, and an associated handler function, then call that handler by specifying the custom event name as the argument to the **trigger()** method.

4 Now, in the script block, insert statements that recognize mouse events by passing data to the event-handler
```
$( "#box" ).on( "mouseenter" ,
  { action: "Mouse Enter" , bg: "Lime" } , handler ) ;
$( "#box" ).on( "mouseleave" ,
  { action: "Mouse Leave" , bg: "Fuchsia" } , handler ) ;
```

5 Finally, insert statements that recognize button events by triggering the mouse event handlers and appending text
```
$( "#entr-btn" ).on( "click" , function() {
  $( "#box" ).trigger( "mouseenter" ) ;
  $( "#out" ).append( " Triggered" ) ; } ) ;

$( "#exit-btn" ).on( "click" , function() {
  $( "#box" ).trigger( "mouseleave" ) ;
  $( "#out" ).append( " Triggered" ) ; } ) ;
```

6 Save the document alongside the jQuery library file then open it in a browser and roll the mouse over the division to see the responses from its mouse event-handlers

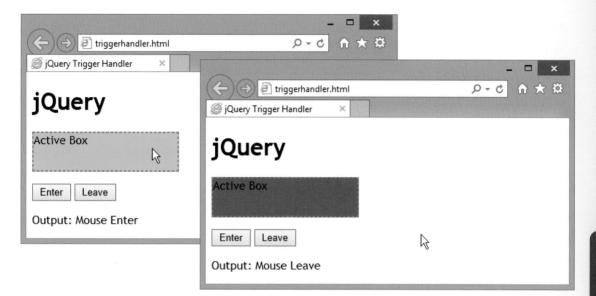

7 Click the buttons in turn to see their own event-handlers provide responses from mouse event-handlers and append text to their output in the span

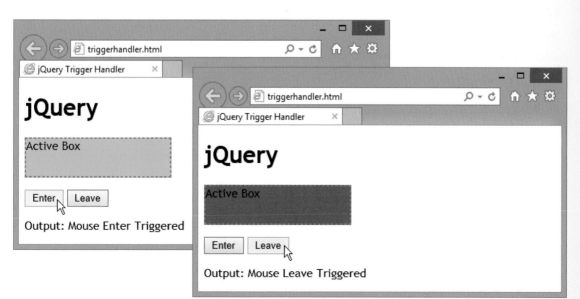

Removing handlers

Just as an event-handler can be nominated for a particular event by the jQuery object's **on()** method, a previously nominated event-handler can be removed by that object's **off()** method. A single event-handler can be nominated or removed for a comma-separated list of multiple event names with these methods:

removehandler.html

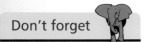

Don't forget

The **off()** method is the recommended way to remove event-handlers and is preferred over the older jQuery **unbind()** and **undelegate()** methods.

Hot tip

You can omit the handler name argument in the **off()** method to remove all its event-handlers, or specify just one event name argument to remove the event-handler for just that event.

1. Add a division plus a paragraph containing two buttons to the body of an HTML document
```
<div id = "box" >Active Box</div>
<p>     <button id = "on-btn" >On</button>
        <button id = "off-btn" >Off</button> </p>
```

2. In the head section of the HTML document add a style sheet to specify initial rules for the division
```
<style>
#box { border:2px dashed gray; width:200px; height:50px; }
</style>
```

3. Next, in the head section of the document, add a script block that defines an event-handler to use variable values
```
$( document ).ready( function() {

  var num = 0 , hue = null , box = $( "#box" ) ;

  function run( ){
    num++ ;
    hue = (num % 2 === 0 ) ? "aqua" : "yellow" ;
    $( this ).css( "background" , hue ) ;
    $( this ).text( "Border Crossing  #" + num ) ; }
    // Nomination statements to be inserted here.
} ) ;
```

4. Now, in the script block, insert a statement to nominate the event-handler for mouse events over the division
```
$( "#on-btn" ).on( "click" , function() {
    box.on( "mouseenter mouseleave" , run ) ;
    box.css( "background" , "lime" ) ;          } ) ;
```

5. Finally, insert a statement to remove the event-handler nominated for mouse events over the division
```
$( "#off-btn" ).on( "click" , function() {
    box.off( "mouseenter mouseleave" , run ) ;
    box.css( "background" , "fuchsia" ) ;         } ) ;
```

6   Save the document alongside the jQuery library file then
     open it in a browser and click the On button – roll the
     mouse over the division to see the event-handler response

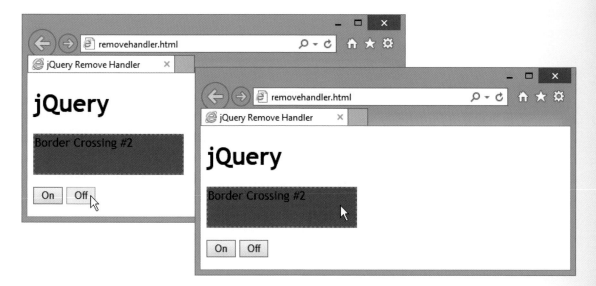

7   Click the Off button then roll the mouse over the
     division to see that the removed event-handler no longer
     responds to the mouse actions

Registering callbacks

A "callback" is simply a function passed as an argument to another function that is expected to call back the received function later. Typically, the simple call back will pass back a value to the caller:

simple.html

1. Add a button and a paragraph containing a span to the body of an HTML document
```
<button id = "btn" >Call</button>
<p>Output: <span id = "out" ></span></p>
```

2. In the head section of the HTML document add a script block that defines a function, which displays a received value then calls back a received function
```
$( document ).ready( function() {
  function process( arg , callback ) {
    $( "#out" ).html( "<br>From Caller: " + arg ) ;
    callback( 2 ) ;  }
} ) ;
```

Beware

When passing a function as an argument, only the name of the function being passed is specified as the argument name – without trailing () parentheses.

3. Next, in the script block, insert a statement that specifies an event-handler, which passes a value and a callback function then displays a value received back
```
$( "#btn" ).on( "click" , function() {
  process( 1 , function( num ) {
  $( "#out" ).append( "<br>From Callback: " + num ) ; } ) ;
} ) ;
```

4. Save the document alongside the jQuery library file then open it in a browser and click the button to see response

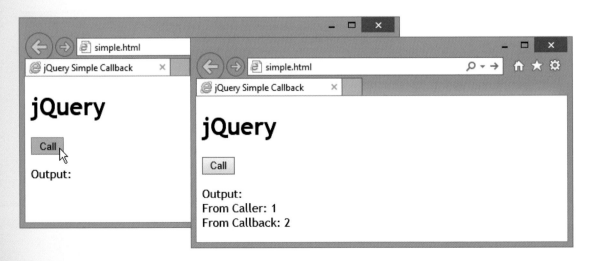

A list of multiple callback functions can usefully be registered in a jQuery Callbacks object. This object is created by the **$.Callbacks()** constructor and each callback function registered using that object's **add()** method. Calling the object's **fire()** method will then execute each callback function in turn:

 Add a button and a paragraph containing a span to the body of an HTML document
```
<button id = "btn" >Call</button>
<p>Output: <span id = "out" ></span></p>
```

callbacks.html

2 In the head section of the HTML document add a script block that creates a callbacks list, containing two functions that each accept a single argument
```
$( document ).ready( function() {
  var callbacks = $.Callbacks() ;
  callbacks.add( function( str ) { $( "#out" ).text( str ) ; } ) ;
  callbacks.add( function( str ) { alert( str ) ; } ) ;
} ) ;
```

Hot tip

The Callbacks object also provides other methods for managing the registered list of callbacks such as **disable()**, **lock()**, **empty()**, and **remove()**.

3 Next, in the script block, insert a statement that specifies an event-handler that calls each callback function
```
$( "#btn" ).on( "click" , function() {
  callbacks.fire( "Hello from the Callbacks List!" ) ;
} ) ;
```

4 Save the document alongside the jQuery library file then open it in a browser and click the button to see response

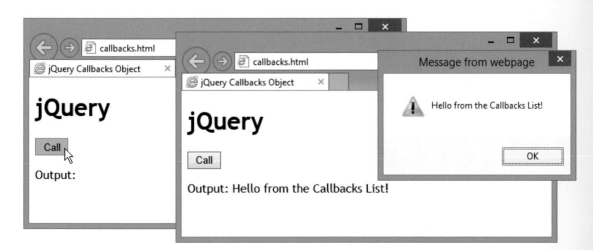

Deferring callbacks

As an alternative to registering multiple callback functions in a Callbacks object, as described on the previous page, callbacks can be attached to a jQuery Deferred object. This can usefully indicate the success or failure of any called synchronous or asynchronous function by firing an appropriate attached callback.

The **$.Deferred()** constructor creates a Deferred object that has **done()**, **fail()**, and **always()** methods, which can each accept a callback function as their argument for attachment to the object.

Deferred objects provide a **resolve()** method to indicate success, that in turn calls the **done()** method – firing its attached callback. Deferred objects also provide a **reject()** method to indicate failure, that in turn calls the **fail()** method – firing its attached callback. Additionally, the optional **always()** method fires its attached callback after the Deferred object has been resolved or rejected.

Optionally, the **resolve()** and **reject()** methods can accept an argument to pass to the relevant attached callback when called.

Calling a Deferred object's **state()** method at any time returns a string representing the current state of the object as either "pending", "resolved", or "rejected":

Don't forget

With Deferred objects, resolve to get the task done, or reject it to fail.

deferred.html

1. Add a button and a paragraph containing a span to the body of an HTML document
```
<button id = "btn" >Call</button>
<p>Output: <span id = "out" ></span></p>
```

2. In the head section of the HTML document add a script block that first specifies an event-handler with variables to store a Deferred object and a reference to the span
```
$( document ).ready( function() {

  $( "#btn" ).on( "click" , function() {
    var dfd = null , out = $( "#out" ) ;
    // Statements to be added here.
  } ) ;
} ) ;
```

3. Next, in the function block, add statements to create a Deferred object and to display its initial state
```
dfd = $.Deferred() ;
out.text( dfd.state() ) ;
```

4 Now, in the function block, add statements to attach callback functions to the Deferred object

```
dfd.done( function( n ) { out.text( this.state() ) ; } ) ;
dfd.fail( function( n ) { out.text( this.state() ) ; } ) ;
dfd.always( function( n ) { out.append( " " + n ) ; } ) ;
```

Don't forget

Optionally, the callbacks could be specified in a chained statement with **dfd.done().fail().always()** but are shown here separately for clarity.

5 Finally, in the function block, add statements to create a 1-second timer that resolves or rejects the Deferred object according to the parity of a selected random number

```
setTimeout( function() {
  var n = Math.ceil( Math.random() * 100 ) ;
  ( n % 2 !== 0 ) ? dfd.reject( n ) : dfd.resolve( n ) ;
} , 1000 ) ;
```

6 Save the document alongside the jQuery library file then open it in a browser and click the button to see a resolved or rejected response from the Deferred object

Hot tip

The Deferred object also provides other methods for managing callbacks such as **then()**, **progress()**, and **notify()**.

111

Keeping promises

Deferred objects become more useful when they are encapsulated within a function that creates the object, calls a function to determine success or failure, then returns a version ("promise") of the object to the caller – relaying its state as "resolved" or "rejected". This allows the caller to attach callback functions to the returned promise object that will be executed according to its state.

Each Deferred object has a **promise()** method that will return a Promise object of itself when called. A Promise object has **done()**, **fail()**, and **always()** methods, to which callbacks can be specified as arguments, but not **resolve()** or **reject()** methods.

The jQuery **$.when()** method accepts a Promise object argument so that callback functions can then be attached upon completion – thus allowing different callbacks to be attached by each caller:

1. Add two buttons and a paragraph containing a span to the body of an HTML document
   ```
   <button id = "get-btn" >Call</button>
   <button id = "eval-btn">Parity</button>
   <p>Output: <span id = "out" ></span></p>
   ```

2. In the head section of the HTML document add a script block that first specifies variables to store a Deferred object and a reference to the span
   ```
   $( document ).ready( function() {

     var dfd = null , out = $( "#out" ) ;
     // Functions and statements to be added here.
   } ) ;
   ```

3. Next, in the script block, add a function that creates a Deferred object then displays its initial state, a timer that resolves or rejects that object, and returns a final promise
   ```
   function getpromise() {
     dfd = $.Deferred() ;
     out.text( dfd.state() ) ;

     setTimeout( function() {
       var n = Math.ceil( Math.random() * 100 ) ;
       ( n % 2 !== 0 ) ? dfd.reject( n ) : dfd.resolve( n ) ;
       } , 1000 ) ;

     return dfd.promise() ;
   }
   ```

④ Now, in the script block, add statements to attach callback functions to the returned Promise object for each buton

```
$( "#get-btn" ).on( "click" , function () {
  var prm = $.when( getpromise() ) ;
  prm.done( function( n ) { out.text( this.state() ) ; } ) ;
  prm.fail( function( n ) { out.text( this.state() ) ; } ) ;
  prm.always( function( n ) { out.append( "  " + n ) ; } ) ;
} ) ;

$( "#eval-btn" ).on( "click" , function () {
  var prm = $.when( getpromise() ) ;
  prm.done( function( n ) { out.text( n + " Even" ) ; } )
  prm.fail( function( n ) { out.text( n + "  Odd" ) ; } ) ;
} ) ;
```

Don't forget

Optionally, the callbacks could be specified in a chained statement with **prm.done().fail().always()** but are shown here separately for clarity.

⑤ Save the document alongside the jQuery library file then open it in a browser and click the buttons to see different resolved or rejected responses from the Promise object

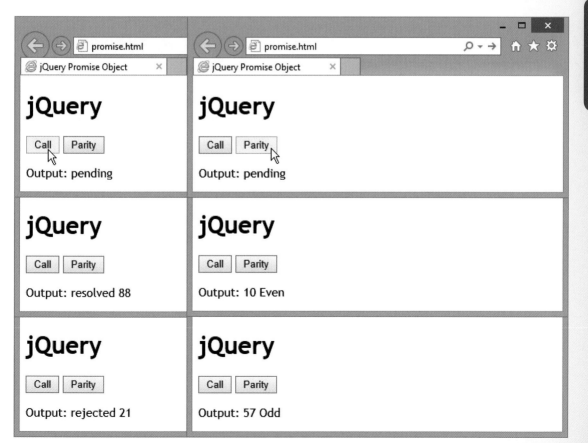

Summary

- Event-handlers can be bound to browser events by specifying event and handler name arguments to the **on()** method

- A handler function bound to an event with the **one()** method will only execute the first time that event fires in the browser

- Multiple event-handlers can be specified to the **on()** method as a JavaScript object defining events and associated handlers

- A data argument can be specified to the **on()** method as a JavaScript object defining key:value pairs for the event object

- Passing an event object to a handler enables stored values to be referenced using the event object's **data** property and keys

- An event-handler bound to an element in a jQuery object can be executed remotely by calling the element's **trigger()** method and can be removed by calling that element's **off()** method

- A callback is a function passed as an argument to another function that can call back the received function later

- The jQuery **$.Callbacks()** constructor creates a Callbacks object list in which functions can be registered using its **add()** method and subsequently executed using its **fire()** method

- The jQuery **$.Deferred()** constructor creates a Deferred object in which callbacks can be specified indicating success or failure

- A Deferred object's **resolve()** method fires **done()** upon success, its **reject()** method fires **fail()** upon failure, and its **always()** method always fires upon completion regardless of success

- Calling a Deferred object's **state()** method returns a string describing current state as "pending", "resolved", or "rejected"

- A Deferred object's **promise()** method returns a Promise object to which callbacks can be attached indicating success or failure

- The jQuery **$.when()** method accepts a Promise object argument so callback functions can be attached on completion

7 Producing effects

This chapter demonstrates how to use jQuery methods to produce dynamic effects.

Hiding elements

The visibility of an element in a jQuery object can be dynamically changed using that object's **hide()** and **show()** methods. Simply calling the **hide()** method, without any arguments, will hide a visible element instantly – as if its CSS **display** property was **none**. Calling the **show()** method, without any arguments, will instantly show a hidden element – restoring its CSS **display** property value.

More interestingly, the **hide()** and **show()** methods can optionally accept an argument to specify the speed of the visibility change. The methods will then perform an animation effect changing the width, height, and opacity over the specified duration period. Duration periods can be specified numerically in milliseconds or by keywords "slow" (600 milliseconds) or "fast" (200 milliseconds).

Optionally, a callback function may also be specified as a second argument to the **hide()** and **show()** methods, which will be fired when the animation completes:

visibility.html

116

1. Add a division and a paragraph containing two buttons and a span to the body of an HTML document
```
<div>Buttons Change Visibility</div>
<p> <button id = "hide-btn" >Hide</button>
    <button id = "show-btn" >Show</button>
    <br>Output: <span id = "out" ></span> </p>
```

2. In the head section of the document add a style sheet to specify division properties and paragraph position
```
<style>
div { padding:5px; width:200px; height:30px;
      background:yellow; border:2px dashed gray; }
p { position:absolute;top:120px; }
</style>
```

3. Next, in the head section of the document, add a script block that specifies an event-handler to hide the division when a button gets clicked and display a confirmation
```
$(document).ready( function() {

  $( "#hide-btn" ).on( "click" , function() {

    $( "div" ).hide( "slow" , function() {
      $( "#out" ).text( "Content Hidden" ) ; } ) ;
  } ) ;

} ) ;
```

Now, in the script block, specify an event-handler to show the hidden division when another button gets clicked and display a confirmation

```
$( "#show-btn" ).on( "click" , function() {

  $( "div" ).show( "slow" , function() {
    $( "#out" ).text( "Content Visible" ) ; } ) ;
} ) ;
```

Save the document alongside the jQuery library file then click the "Hide" button to see the animation hide the division and display the confirmation on completion

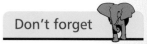
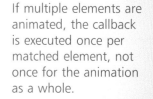
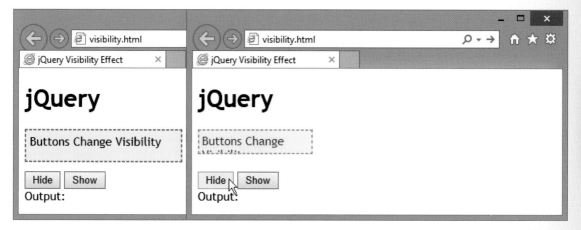

Click the "Show" button to see the animation show the division and display the confirmation on completion

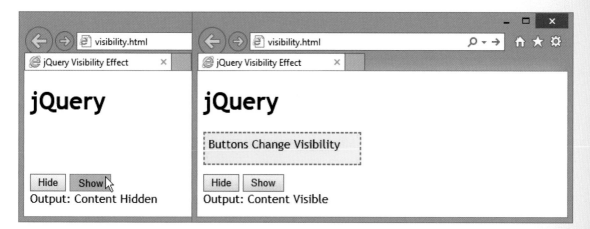

Toggling elements

The visibility of an element in a jQuery object can be dynamically changed using that object's **toggle()** method. Simply calling the **toggle()** method, without any arguments, will instantly hide a visible element or instantly show a hidden element – reversing its current CSS **display** property value.

The **toggle()** method can optionally accept a Boolean argument to explicitly determine the visibility of the element, where **true** is visible and **false** is hidden.

Additionally, the **toggle()** methods can accept an argument to specify the speed of the visibility change. The methods will then perform an animation effect changing the width, height, and opacity over the specified duration period. Duration periods can be specified numerically in milliseconds or by keywords "slow" (600 milliseconds) or "fast" (200 milliseconds).

Optionally, a callback function may also be specified as a second argument to the **toggle()** method, which will be fired when the animation completes:

Hot tip

All jQuery animation effects can be turned off by adding the statement **$.fx.off = true** at the start of the script block.

toggle.html

Don't forget

In this example, the Show button will only display the division when it is already hidden – when its CSS **display** property has a value of **none**.

1. Add a division and a paragraph containing two buttons and a span to the body of an HTML document

```
<div>Button Toggles Visibility</div>
<p> <button id = "tog-btn" >Toggle</button>
        <button id = "show-btn" >Show</button>
    <br>Output: <span id = "out" ></span> </p>
```

2. In the head section of the document add a style sheet to specify division properties and paragraph position

```
<style>
div { padding:5px; width:200px; height:30px;
        background:lime; border:2px dashed gray; }
p { position:absolute;top:120px; }
</style>
```

3. Next, in the head section of the document, add a script block that specifies an event-handler to show the division if hidden when a button gets clicked

```
$(document).ready( function() {

  $( "#show-btn" ).on( "click" , function() {
    $( "div" ).toggle( true ) ;
    $( "#out" ).text( "Content Visible" ) ; } ) ;
} ) ;
```

4   Now, in the script block, specify an event-handler to toggle visibility of the division when another button gets clicked and display a confirmation

```
$( "#tog-btn" ).on( "click" , function() {

  $( "div" ).toggle( "slow" , function() {
    if ( $( "div" ).css( "display" ) == "none" )
                  $( "#out" ).text( "Content Hidden" ) ;
    else          $( "#out" ).text( "Content Visible" ) ; } ) ;
} ) ;
```

Hot tip

Double-click this Toggle button to see the division hide then show as jQuery queues the function calls.

5   Save the document alongside the jQuery library file then click the buttons to see the animation hide and show the division, and display confirmation on each completion

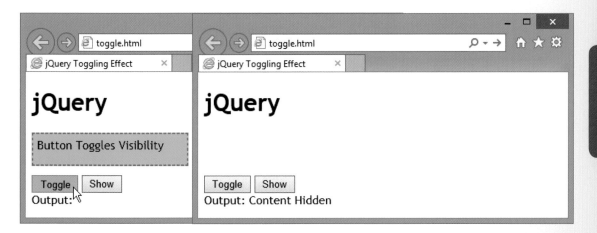

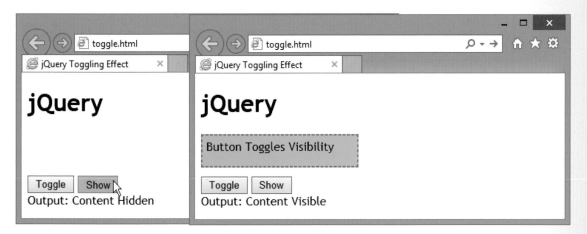

Sliding elements

The visibility of an element in a jQuery object can be dynamically changed using that object's **slideUp()**, **slideDown()**, and **slideToggle()** methods to perform an animation from visible to hidden, and back from hidden to visible.

The **slideUp()**, **slideDown()**, and **slideToggle()** methods accept an argument to specify the speed of the visibility change. These methods will then perform an animation, vertically sliding the element's visibility over the specified duration period. Duration periods can be specified numerically in milliseconds or by keywords "slow" (600 milliseconds) or "fast" (200 milliseconds).

Optionally, a callback function may be specified as a second argument to the **slideUp()**, **slideDown()**, and **slideToggle()** methods, which will be fired when the animation completes:

slide.html

1   Add a division and a paragraph containing three buttons and a span to the body of an HTML document
```
<div>Buttons Slide Visibility</div>
<p>      <button id = "up-btn" >Up</button>
         <button id = "dn-btn" >Down</button>
         <button id = "tog-btn" >Toggle</button>
<br>Output: <span id = "out" ></span> </p>
```

2   In the head section of the document add a style sheet to specify division properties and paragraph position
```
<style>
div { padding:5px; width:200px; height:30px;
        background:aqua; border:2px dashed gray; }
p { position:absolute;top:120px; }
</style>
```

3   Next, in the head section of the document, add a script block that specifies an event-handler to hide the division when a button gets clicked and display a confirmation
```
$(document).ready( function() {

  $( "#up-btn" ).on( "click" , function() {

    $( "div" ).slideUp( "slow" , function() {
      $( "#out" ).text( "Content Hidden" ) ; } ) ;
  } ) ;

  } ) ;
```

Beware

Notice that these function names must be correctly capitalized using camelCase, not simply all lowercase – for example **slideUp()** rather than **slideup()**.

④ Now, in the script block, specify an event-handler to show the hidden division when another button gets clicked and display a confirmation

```
$( "#dn-btn" ).on( "click" , function() {

  $( "div" ).slideDown( "slow" , function() {
    $( "#out" ).text( "Content Visible" ) ; } ) ;
} ) ;
```

Hot tip

These animations change the element's visibility by dynamically adjusting its CSS **height** property.

⑤ Finally, in the script block, specify an event-handler to toggle visibility of the division when another button gets clicked and display a confirmation

```
$( "#tog-btn" ).on( "click" , function() {

  $( "div" ).slideToggle( "slow" , function() {
    if ( $( "div" ).css( "display" ) === "none" )
    $( "#out" ).text( "Content Hidden" ) ;
    else $( "#out" ).text( "Content Visible" ) ; } ) ;
  } ) ;
```

⑥ Save the document alongside the jQuery library file then click the buttons to see the animations hide or show the division and display the confirmation on each completion

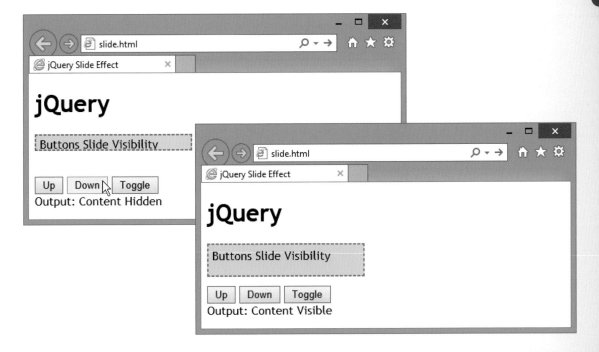

Fading content

The visibility of an element in a jQuery object can be dynamically changed using that object's **fadeIn()**, **fadeOut()**, and **fadeToggle()** methods to perform an animation from visible to hidden, and back from hidden to visible.

The **fadeIn()**, **fadeOut()**, and **fadeToggle()** methods accept an argument to specify the speed of the visibility change. These methods will then perform an animation uniformly reducing the element's opacity over the specified duration period. Duration periods can be specified numerically in milliseconds or by keywords "slow" (600 milliseconds) or "fast" (200 milliseconds).

Optionally, a callback function may be specified as a second argument to the **fadeIn()**, **fadeOut()**, and **fadeToggle()** methods, which will be fired when the animation completes:

fade.html

1 Add a division and a paragraph containing three buttons and a span to the body of an HTML document

```
<div>Buttons Fade Visibility</div>
<p>      <button id = "out-btn" >Fade Out</button>
         <button id = "in-btn" >Fade In</button>
         <button id = "tog-btn" >Toggle</button>
<br>Output: <span id = "out" ></span> </p>
```

2 In the head section of the document add a style sheet to specify division properties and paragraph position

```
<style>
div { padding:5px; width:200px; height:30px;
        background:fuchsia; border:2px dashed gray; }
p { position:absolute;top:120px; }
</style>
```

3 Next, in the head section of the document, add a script block that specifies an event-handler to hide the division when a button gets clicked and display a confirmation

```
$(document).ready( function() {

  $( "#out-btn" ).on( "click" , function() {

    $( "div" ).fadeOut( "slow" , function() {
      $( "#out" ).text( "Content Hidden" ) ; } ) ;
  } ) ;

} ) ;
```

Beware

Notice that these function names must be correctly capitalized using camelCase, not simply all lowercase – for example **fadeIn()** rather than **fadein()**.

4 Now, in the script block, specify an event-handler to show the hidden division when another button gets clicked and display a confirmation

```
$( "#in-btn" ).on( "click" , function() {

  $( "div" ).fadeIn( "slow" , function() {
    $( "#out" ).text( "Content Visible" ) ; } ) ;
} ) ;
```

Hot tip

These animations change the element's visibility by dynamically adjusting its CSS **opacity** property.

5 Finally, in the script block, specify an event-handler to toggle visibility of the division when another button gets clicked and display a confirmation

```
$( "#tog-btn" ).on( "click" , function() {

  $( "div" ).fadeToggle( "slow" , function() {
    if ( $( "div" ).css( "display" ) === "none" )
    $( "#out" ).text( "Content Hidden" ) ;
    else $( "#out" ).text( "Content Visible" ) ; } ) ;
} ) ;
```

6 Save the document alongside the jQuery library file then click the buttons to see the animations hide or show the division and display the confirmation on each completion

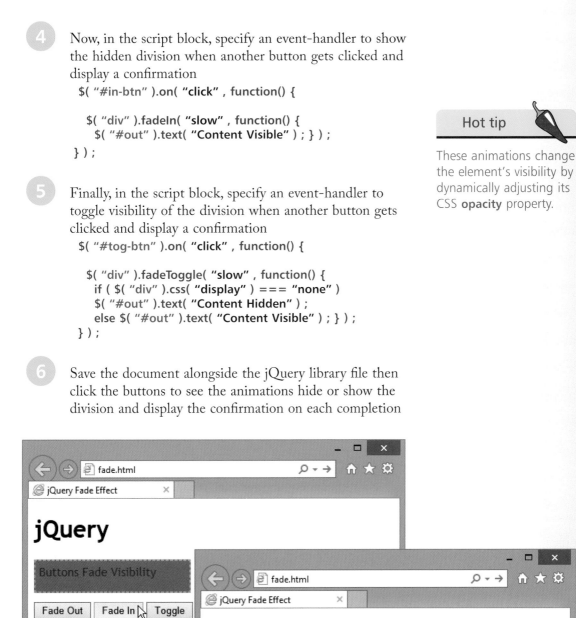

Fading to levels

As an alternative to fading the visibility of an element in a jQuery object using that object's **fadeIn()**, **fadeOut()**, and **fadeToggle()** methods, described on the previous page, its visibility can be faded to a specified level of opacity using the object's **fadeTo()** method.

The **fadeTo()** method accepts a first argument to specify the speed of the visibility change, either numerically in milliseconds or by keywords "slow" (600 milliseconds) or "fast" (200 milliseconds), and a second argument to specify the level of opacity at which to stop fading in the range 0.0 (hidden) to 1.0 (maximum). This method performs an animation that reduces the element's opacity over the specified duration period to the specified level of opacity.

Optionally, a callback function may be specified as a third argument to the **fadeTo()** method, which will be fired when the animation completes:

fadeto.html

1. Add a division and a paragraph containing two buttons and a span to the body of an HTML document
```
<div>Buttons Fade To Levels</div>
<p>     <button id = "btn25" >Quarter</button>
         <button id = "btn100" >Maximum</button>
<br>Output: <span id = "out" ></span>          </p>
```

2. In the head section of the document add a style sheet to specify division properties and paragraph position
```
<style>
div { padding:5px; width:200px; height:30px;
          background:black; color:white; }
p { position:absolute;top:120px; }
</style>
```

3. Next, in the head section of the document, add a script block that specifies an event-handler to fade down the division on a button click and display a confirmation
```
$(document).ready( function() {

  $( "#btn25" ).on( "click" , function() {

    $( "div" ).fadeTo( "slow" , 0.25 , function() {
      $( "#out" ).text( "Silver - 25%" ) ; } ) ;
  } ) ;

} ) ;
```

Beware

The function name must be correctly capitalized using camelCase as **fadeTo()**, not as **fadeto()**.

④ Now, in the script block, specify an event-handler to fade up the division when another button gets clicked and display a confirmation

```
$( "#btn100" ).on( "click" , function() {

    $( "div" ).fadeTo( "slow" , 1.0 , function() {
        $( "#out" ).text( "Black - 100%" ) ; }
    ) ;
} ) ;
```

Hot tip

If the duration argument is omitted from any fade method the default of 400 milliseconds is used.

⑤ Save the document alongside the jQuery library file then click the buttons to see the animations fade the division and display confirmation on each completion

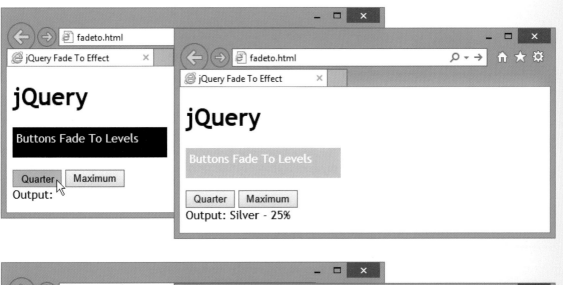

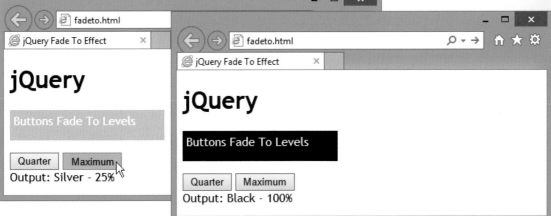

Animating elements

Any numeric CSS property of an element in a jQuery object can be dynamically changed using that object's **animate()** method to perform animation effects.

The **animate()** method accepts as its first argument a JavaScript object of key:value pairs specifying CSS properties and values, and a second argument to specify the duration of the animation. Duration periods can be specified numerically in milliseconds or by keywords "slow" (600 milliseconds) or "fast" (200 milliseconds).

Optionally, a callback function may be specified as a third argument to the **animate()** method, which will be fired when the animation completes:

animate.html

1. Add a division and a paragraph containing one button and a span to the body of an HTML document
```
<div>Button Animates Content</div>
<p>    <button id = "btn" >Animate</button>
         <br>Output: <span id = "out" ></span></p>
```

2. In the head section of the document add a style sheet to specify division properties and paragraph position
```
<style>
div , p { position:absolute; left:10px; top:120px; }
div { top:80px; padding:5px; width:200px; height:30px;
         background:fuchsia; border:2px dashed gray; }
</style>
```

3. Next, in the head section of the document, add a script block that initializes a global variable to toggle animations
```
$(document).ready( function() {

    var tog = false ;

} ) ;
```

4. Now, in the script block, add a function to display the current horizontal position of an element when called
```
function report( ) {
  $( "#out" ).text( "Done. Left Now " +
                                  $( this ).css( "left" ) ) ;
}
```

5 Finally, in the script block, specify an event-handler to test the variable then horizontally animate the division when the button gets clicked and display a confirmation

```
$( "#btn" ).on( "click" , function() {
  tog = !tog ;
  if ( tog )
  $( "div" ).animate( { left : "100px" } , "slow", report ) ;
  else
  $( "div" ).animate( { left : "10px" } , "slow", report ) ;
} ) ;
```

Beware

Animation gets performed on CSS properties so elements to be animated must have an existing **position** property value of **absolute**, **fixed**, or **relative**.

6 Save the document alongside the jQuery library file then click the buttons to see the animation and position confirmation on each completion

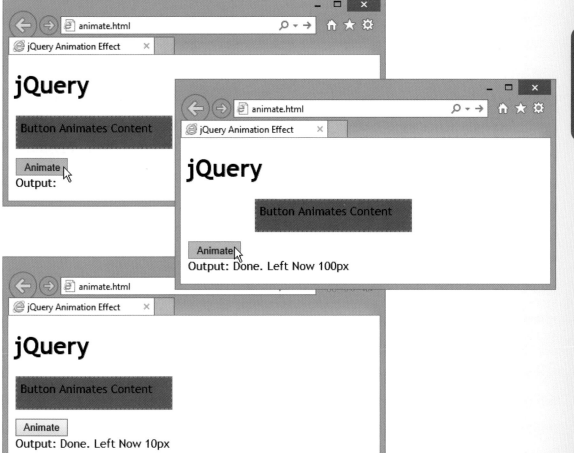

Stopping animations

An animation currently running on an element in a jQuery object can be stopped immediately by calling that object's **stop()** method. For example, an element that is in the process of becoming hidden by the **slideToggle()** method when **stop()** is called will remain visible, but at a fraction of its previous height.

The **stop()** method can simply be called without any arguments. Optionally, a comma-separated pair of Boolean arguments can be supplied to specify if any further animations should be cleared and if the current animation should jump to its end point. If not supplied, the default values for these "clearQueue" and "jumpToEnd" arguments are in each case **false**, but specifying a **true** value will jump to the end of the current animation:

1. Add a division and a paragraph containing three buttons and a span to the body of an HTML document

```
<div>Buttons Control Animation</div>
<p>      <button id = "run-btn" >Run</button>
         <button id = "stop-btn" >Stop</button>
         <button id = "end-btn" >End</button>
<br>Output: <span id = "out" ></span></p>
```

2. In the head section of the document add a style sheet to specify division properties and paragraph position

```
<style>
div { padding:5px; width:200px; height:30px;
background:lime; border:2px dashed gray; }
p { position:absolute;top:120px; }
</style>
```

3. Next, in the head section of the document, add a script block that specifies an event-handler for the first button – which runs an animation, displays a confirmation, and ensures the other two buttons are enabled

```
$(document).ready( function() {

  $( "#run-btn" ).on( "click" , function() {
    $( "div" ).slideToggle( 2000 ) ;
    $( "#out" ).text( "Running..." ) ;
    $( "#stop-btn , #end-btn" ).removeAttr( "disabled" ) ;
  } ) ;

} ) ;
```

stop.html

128

Don't forget

If the jumpToEnd argument is provided with a value of **true**, the current animation stops and the element is immediately given its target values for the specified CSS property.

④ Now, in the script block, specify event-handlers for the other two buttons – which stop the animation, display a confirmation, and modify button enablement

```
$( "#stop-btn" ).on( "click" , function() {
  $( "div" ).stop() ;
  $( "#out" ).text( "Stopped At "+$( "div" ).css( "height" ) ) ;
  $( "#end-btn" ).attr( "disabled" , "true" ) ; } ) ;

$( "#end-btn" ).on( "click" , function() {
  $( "div" ).stop( true , true ) ;
  $( "#out" ).text( "Done" ) ;
  $( "#stop-btn" ).attr( "disabled" , "true" ) ; } ) ;
```

Beware

Callback functions are not called when the **stop()** function is called.

⑤ Save the document alongside the jQuery library file then click the buttons to see the animation run and stop

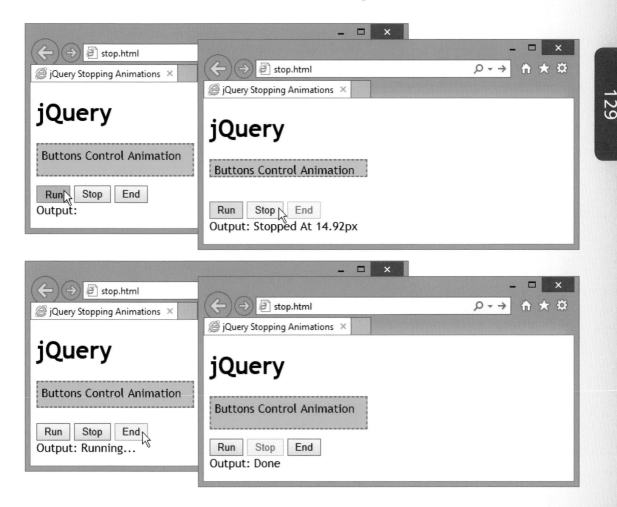

Handling queues

Multiple animations assigned to an element in a jQuery object get placed in a queue, to be executed in sequence after the first animation in that sequence completes. The default jQuery queue is named "fx" and can be referenced by the object's **queue()** method. This has a **length** property that contains an integer denoting the number of animations remaining in the current queue.

Queued animations can be paused by specifying a duration argument in milliseconds to an element object's **delay()** method.

Execution of all animations in a queue can be immediately terminated by calling the element object's **finish()** method – stopping the currently-running animation, removing all queued animations, and finishing at the end point of the final animation:

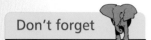

Don't forget

Unlike **stop(true, true)** the **finish()** method jumps to the CSS values of the final animation.

queue.html

1. Add a division and a paragraph containing three buttons and a span to the body of an HTML document
```
<div>Buttons Control Queue</div>
<p>    <button id = "run-btn" >Run</button>
         <button id = "fin-btn" >Finish</button>
<br>Output: <span id = "out" ></span></p>
```

2. In the head section of the document add a style sheet to specify division properties and paragraph position
```
<style>
div , p { position:absolute; left:10px; top:120px; }
div { top:80px; padding:5px; width:200px; height:30px;
background:aqua; border:2px dashed gray; }
</style>
```

Hot tip

You can also call **dequeue()** to execute the next animation on a queue and **clearQueue()** to remove all remaining animations in a queue.

3. Next, in the head section of the document, add a script block defining a timer function to display queue length
```
$(document).ready( function() {

  var div = $( "div" ) ;

  function count() {
    $( "#out" ).text( "Queue Length " + div.queue().length ) ;
    setTimeout( count, 100 ) ; }

} ) ;
```

4. Now, in the script block, specify an event-handler to terminate the queue when a button gets clicked
```
$( "#fin-btn" ).on( "click" , function() { div.finish() ; } ) ;
```

⑤ Finally, in the script block, specify an event-handler to
run an animation queue and start the timer when the
other button gets clicked

```
$( "#run-btn" ).on( "click" , function() {
  div.animate( { left: "200" } , 2000 ) ;
  div.slideUp( 2000 ).delay( 1000 ).slideDown( 2000 ) ;
  div.animate( { left: "10" } , 2000 ) ;
  count() ;
} ) ;
```

Hot tip

Notice how the slide
and delay animations are
chained together into a
single statement here.

⑥ Save the document alongside the jQuery library file then
click the buttons to see the animations run and finish

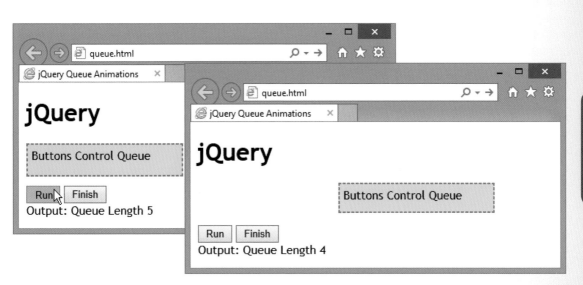

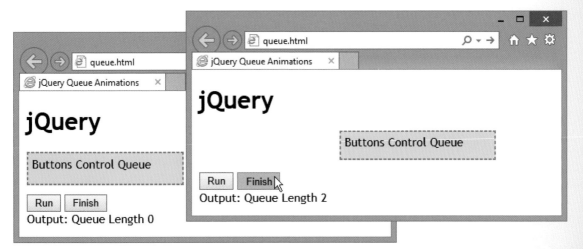

Summary

- Visibility of an element in a jQuery object can be changed using that object's **hide()** and **show()** methods

- Animation effects must specify a duration argument, expressed in milliseconds or using the keywords "fast" or "slow"

- Optionally, a final callback function argument can be specified to be called on completion of an animation effect

- The **toggle()** method reverses the current CSS **display** property or can accept a Boolean value to explicitly determine visibility

- The **slideUp()**, **slideDown()**, and **slideToggle()** animation effect methods change the visible CSS **height** property

- The **fadeIn()**, **fadeOut()**, and **fadeToggle()** animation effect methods change the visible CSS **opacity** property

- The level of opacity at which to stop fading is specified as an argument in the range 0.0 to 1.0 with the **fadeTo()** method

- Any numeric CSS property of an element in a jQuery object can be dynamically changed by that object's **animate()** method

- CSS properties and values are specified as key:value pairs in a JavaScript object as the first argument to the **animate()** method

- An animation currently running on an element object can be immediately stopped by calling that object's **stop()** method

- The **stop()** method can accept a pair of Boolean values to explicitly determine "clearQueue" and "jumpToEnd" properties

- Multiple animations assigned to an element in a jQuery object get placed in a default queue named "fx"

- The **length** property of the **queue()** method contains an integer denoting the number of animations remaining in the queue

- Queued animations can be paused by the **delay()** method and the entire queue can be terminated by the **finish()** method

8 Employing AJAX

This chapter demonstrates how to update page content with asynchronous AJAX requests to the web server.

Loading content

AJAX (<u>A</u>synchronous <u>J</u>avaScript <u>a</u>nd <u>X</u>ML) techniques enable data to be exchanged with the web server as a background (asynchronous) process and so allow content to be inserted into a web page without updating the entire page.

Data can easily be requested from the web server using jQuery AJAX methods to retrieve text, HTML, XML, or JSON objects. Existing content of an element in a jQuery object can be replaced with new data from the web server simply by specifying the URL address of the data to that object's **load()** method.

The examples in this chapter use the free Abyss Personal Edition web server available from www.aprelium.com

Internally, when the **load()** method has successfully retrieved the specified data it is, by default, passed internally to the **html()** method for insertion into the web page. This means that all HTML markup and CSS styles within the data are parsed by the browser and preserved when the new content appears on the page:

load.txt

1   Create a plain text document containing text snippets enclosed within HTML markup tags that specify inline CSS styles and a local image file named "abyss.png"
```
<p style="background:aqua">
<span id="content" style="background:yellow">
Web Server content </span>
supplied by AJAX Response</p>
<img src="abyss.png">
```

2   Save the text document as a file named **load.txt** in the documents directory of your web server – typically named "htdocs" (for example at **C:\Abyss Web Server\htdocs**)

load.html

3   Next, add a division and a paragraph containing a button to the body of an HTML document
```
<div>Push The Load Button To Request Content</div>
<p><button id = "btn" >Load</button></p>
```

4   Now, in the head section of the HTML document, add a script block that specifies an event-handler for the button
```
$(document).ready( function() {

  $( "#btn" ).on( "click" , function() {
    $( "div" ).load( "load.txt" ) ;
  } ) ;

} ) ;
```

5 Finally, save the document in your web server's documents directory (**htdocs**) alongside the text document, the jQuery library file, and the image file

load.html   jquery-xxx.min.js   load.txt   abyss.png

6 Ensure that your web server is running, then open the web page in your browser and push the button to send the request – see the content get dynamically replaced

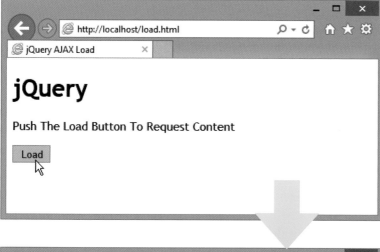

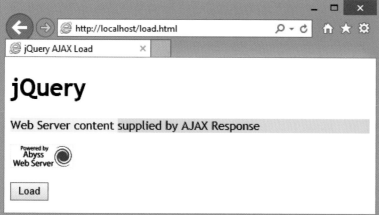

Beware

All examples in this chapter must be loaded via a webserver to use HTTP – they will not execute simply by opening them directly in your web browser.

Hot tip

A locally installed web server can usually be addressed via HTTP using the domain name **localhost** or using the IP address **127.0.0.1**.

Don't forget

Browser security restrictions only permit AJAX requests via HTTP on the same domain – you cannot retrieve data from another web server.

Loading spans

The argument to the **load()** method simply specifies the URL of a remote document to be retrieved from the web server. This can optionally be extended by adding a jQuery selector to specify a fragment of the remote document to be inserted in the web page. The selector must be added after the URL and a space character. For example, an ID selector could be added to specify a particular span element in the remote document for insertion into the page.

When content has been inserted into a web page by AJAX, the original state of the page cannot be restored by the browser's Back button, which loads the previous page. It can, therefore, be useful to store replaced original content so the user may restore it later:

loadspan.html

1 Add a division plus a paragraph containing two buttons and a span to the body of an HTML document

```
<div>Push The Load Button To Request Content<div>
<p>      <button id = "btn" >Load</button>
         <button id = "rtn" >Unload</button><br>
Output: <span id = "out" >???</span></p>
```

2 Now, in the head section of the HTML document, add a script block that initializes a variable with original content

```
$(document).ready( function() {

   var store = $( "#out" ).html() ;
   // Statements to be added here.

} ) ;
```

Beware

Note that the string argument in the **load()** method separately specifies a file name and a selector – which must be separated by a space.

3 Next, in the script block, add a statement specifying an event-handler that replaces the original span content with content from a specific span in a retrieved file

```
$( "#btn" ).on( "click" , function() {

   $( "#out" ).load( "load.txt #content" ) ;
} ) ;
```

4 Finally, in the script block, add a statement specifying an event-handler that restores the original span content

```
$( "#rtn" ).on( "click" , function() {

   $( "#out" ).html( store ) ;
} ) ;
```

5 Save the document on the web server, alongside the jQuery library file and text file created in the previous example, then open the web page in your browser and push buttons to see span content replaced and restored

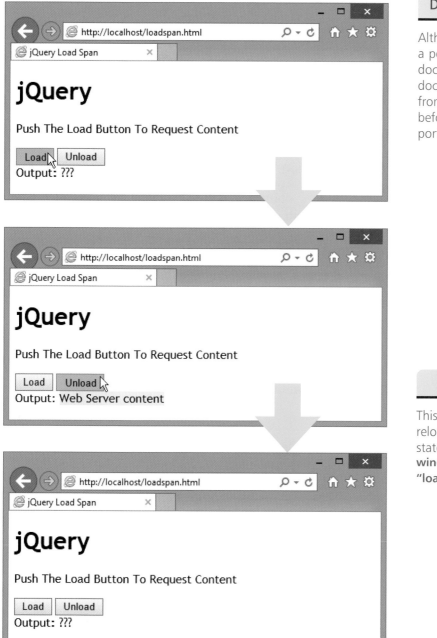

Don't forget

Although only inserting a portion of the remote document, that entire document gets retrieved from the web server before jQuery selects the portion to be inserted.

Hot tip

This entire page can be reloaded to its original state with pure JavaScript **window.location.ref = "loadspan.html"**.

Testing loads

Optionally, a callback function can be specified as an additional argument to the **load()** method to receive these three parameters:

- **responseTxt** – actual returned content when the call succeeds

- **statusTxt** – a string describing the status of the call

- **xhr** – the <u>XMLH</u>ttp<u>R</u>equest object

The **statusTxt** string can be examined to test whether the content loaded successfully and **statusText** and **status** properties of the XMLHttpRequest **xhr** object can reveal details upon failure:

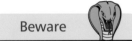

loadtest.html

1 Add a division plus a paragraph containing two buttons and a span to the body of an HTML document

```
<div>Push The Load Button To Request Content</div>
<p>      <button id = "btn-a" >Load A</button>
            <button id = "btn-b" >Load B</button>
<br>Output: <span id = "out" ></span></p>
```

2 Now, in the head section of the HTML document, add a script block with a function that assesses load success

```
$(document).ready( function() {

    function assess( statusTxt , xhr ) {
    if( statusTxt == "success" )
      $( "#out" ).text( "External content loaded successfully!" ) ;
    if( statusTxt == "error" ) {
      $( "div" ).text( xhr.statusText ) ;
      $( "#out" ).text( xhr.status ) ; }            }
} ) ;
```

Beware

The **statusTxt** name here merely reflects the nature of the string being passed for assessment and could be renamed, but **xhr.statusText** (with an e) is a property name that cannot be changed.

3 Next, in the script block, add statements specifying event-handlers that attempt to load content and assess results

```
$( "#btn-a" ).on( "click" , function() {
    $( "div" ).load( "load.txt #content" ,
      function( responseTxt , statusTxt , xhr )
      { assess( statusTxt , xhr ) ; } ) ;
} ) ;

$( "#btn-b" ).on( "click" , function() {
    $( "div" ).load( "none.txt" ,
      function( responseTxt , statusTxt , xhr )
      { assess( statusTxt , xhr ) ; } ) ;
} ) ;
```

4 Save the document on the web server, alongside the jQuery library file and the text file created on page 134, then open the web page in your browser and push the buttons to see the load attempts tested

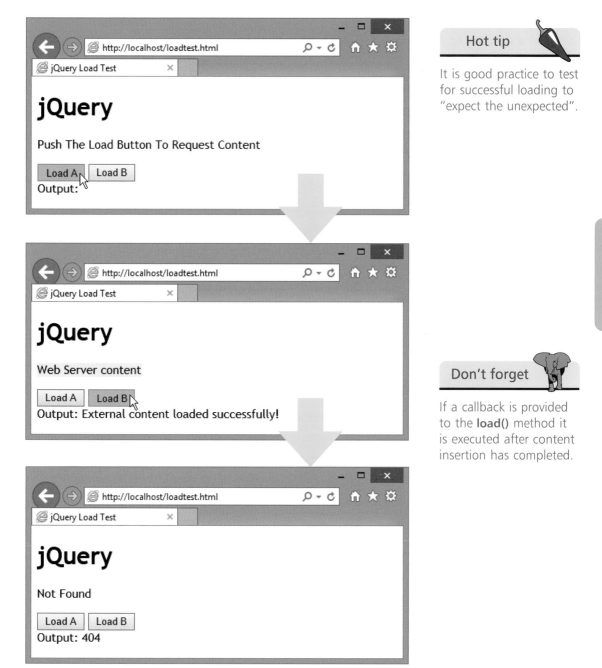

Hot tip

It is good practice to test for successful loading to "expect the unexpected".

Don't forget

If a callback is provided to the **load()** method it is executed after content insertion has completed.

Getting response

The **load()** method, described on the previous pages, uses the HTTP GET and POST methods to retrieve data and send data. These actions can each be implemented explicitly using the jQuery **$.get()** and **$.post()** methods with noteworthy differences:

This example assumes the web server supports PHP scripting. You can discover how to add PHP support to the Abyss web server online at **aprelium.com/abyssws/ php5win.html** and learn server-side scripting with the companion book in this series: PHP & MySQL in easy steps.

Feature:	GET:	POST:
Back Button	Cannot re-send data	Can re-send data
Bookmark-able	Yes	No
Cache-able	Yes	No
History	Parameters saved	Parameters unsaved
Data Length	2048 character limit	Unrestricted
Data Type	Only ASCII text	Unrestricted
Visibility	Data added to URL	Data hidden

The jQuery **$.get()** and **$.post()** methods may each accept four arguments – a required URL to which the request will be sent, optional data in a JavaScript object of key:value pairs or string to be sent, an optional callback function to execute on success, and an optional data type of "text", "html", "xml", "script", or "json". Additionally, JavaScript objects can be retrieved with **$.getJSON()** and scripts retrieved and executed with the **$.getScript()** method:

1 Create a plain text document containing a simple message and save it as a file named **getpost.txt** on the web server
Push Buttons To Get Data

getpost.txt

2 Next, create a script containing a function to display array values and save it as a file named **getpost.js** on the server
function report(a) {
$("#out").text(a.page +" at "+ a.date +" via "+ a.type) ;
}

getpost.js

getpost.php

3 Now, create a server script to return a JavaScript object and save it as a file named **getpost.php** on the web server
<?php date_default_timezone_set('UTC') ;
$p = $_REQUEST['page'] ; $d = date('H:i:s') ;
$t = $_SERVER['REQUEST_METHOD'] ;
echo json_encode(
array("page"=> $p,"date"=> $d , "type"=> $t)) ; ?>

4 Add a paragraph containing two buttons and a paragraph containing a span to the body of an HTML document

```
<p><button id="get-btn">GET</button>
<button id="post-btn">POST</button></p>
<p>Output: <span id="out"></span></p>
```

getpost.html

5 Now, in the head section of the HTML document, add a script block that gets the text and script from the server

```
$(document).ready( function() {

    $.get( "getpost.txt" , function( msg ) {
        $( "#out" ).text( msg ) } ) ;
    $.getScript( "getpost.js" ) ;
    // Event-handler statements to be added here.
} ) ;
```

Hot tip

Most AJAX requests cannot retrieve data from a different domain but script requests can.

6 Finally, in the script block, add statements to specify event-handlers to get data when each button is pushed

```
$( "#get-btn" ).on( "click" , function() {
    $.getJSON( "getpost.php" ,
        { page:document.title } , report ) ; } ) ;

$( "#post-btn" ).on( "click" , function() {
    $.post( "getpost.php" ,
        { page:document.title } , report , "json" ) ; } ) ;
```

Don't forget

JSON (JavaScript Object Notation) is a lightweight data-interchange format. See json.org for details.

7 Save this document on the server, alongside the jQuery library and other files, then push the buttons for response

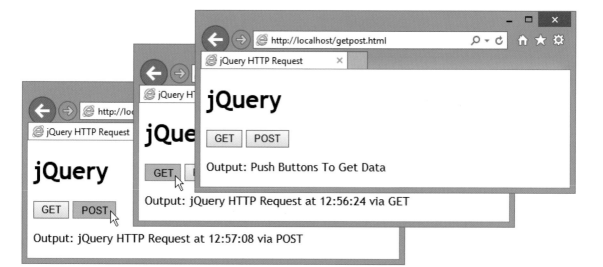

Performing requests

For maximum control when performing AJAX requests jQuery provides an intrinsic **$.ajax()** method. In its simplest form this can accept a single argument specifying a URL to which the request will be sent. But the **$.ajax()** method can also accept a list of key:value "hook" options to control of every aspect of the request:

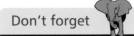

Don't forget

You can use the **load()**, **$.post()**, **$.get()**, **$.getScript()**, and **$getJSON()** methods described on previous pages but the **$.ajax()** method provides more options for finer control.

Hot tip

The XMLHttpRequest (xhr) object has its own methods and properties, such as **readyState**, but these are not often needed with jQuery.

142

Key:	Option Description:
async	Is asynchronous (default true)
beforeSend(*xhr*)	Function to run before submission
cache	Is cache allowed (default true)
complete(*xhr,status*)	Function to run on completion – both after success or failure
contentType	MIME type to use for submission
context	Use "this" for callback functions
data	Data to be sent to the server
dataFilter(*data,type*)	How to handle response data
dataType	MIME type expected for response
error(*xhr,status,error*)	Function to run on failure
global	Is triggering allowed (default true)
ifModified	Is response different (default false)
password	Authentication for HTTP access
processData	Transform to string (default true)
scriptCharset	Character set for the request
success(*result,status,xhr*)	Function to run on success
timeout	Timeout in milliseconds for request
traditional	Is traditional style used to serialize arrays and objects (default false)
type	HTTP request method (default GET)
url	URL to which the request is sent
username	Authentication for HTTP access
xhr	Callback function to create an XMLHttpRequest object

1. Create a plain text document containing a simple message and save it as a file named **ajax.txt** on the web server
This data from AJAX request...

ajax.txt

2. Add a paragraph containing a button and a paragraph containing a span to the body of an HTML document
\<p>\<button id="btn">Send AJAX Request\</button>\</p>
\<p>Output: \<span id = "out" >\</span>\</p>

ajax.html

3. Now, in the head section of the HTML document, add a script block that specifies an event-handler for the button
$(document).ready(function() {

```
$( "#btn" ).on( "click" , function() {
// AJAX request to be added here.
} ) ;

} ) ;
```

4. Next, in the event-handler block, add the AJAX request to display the text document without adding it to cache
```
$.ajax( {
  url: "ajax.txt" ,
  cache: false   ,
  success: function( msg ) { $( "#out" ).text( msg ) ; }   ,
  complete: function(){ $( "#out" ).append( "Done" ) ; }
} ) ;
```

Beware

Remember that each key:value pair must be separated from the next pair by a comma.

5. Save the document on the web server alongside the jQuery library file and text file then open the web page in your browser and push the button to see the AJAX response

Serializing form data

Submission of HTML form data via AJAX is made delightfully simple by the jQuery **serialize()** and **serializeArray()** methods. Calling the **serialize()** method of a form element within a jQuery object creates a single query string ready for submission – encoding the name and value of all that form's valid elements. Similarly, calling the **serializeArray()** method of a form element in a jQuery object creates a single array ready for submission – containing the name and value of all that form's valid elements:

serialform.html

1 Add a form and a paragraph containing two spans to the body of an HTML document
```
<form> <input type="text" name="fname" value="Bugs">
        <input type="text" name="lname" value="Bunny">
<input type="button" id="btn" value="Serialize"></form>
<p>Array... <span id = "arr" ></span>
<br>Query.. <span id = "qry" ></span></p>
```

2 Now, in the head section of the HTML document, add a script block specifying an event-handler to serialize data
```
$(document).ready( function() {

  $( "#btn" ).on( "click" , function() {

  $.each( $( "form" ).serializeArray() , function( i , n ) {
  $( "#arr" ).append(i+"="+n.name+":"+n.value+" ") ; } ) ;
  $( "#qry" ).text( $( "form" ).serialize() ) ;
  } ) ;
} ) ;
```

3 Save this document alongside the jQuery library file then push the button to see serialized form names and values

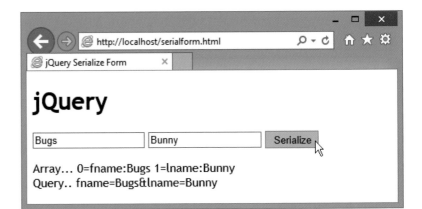

1. Create a server script to return a message containing two serialized values from a submitted form

```php
<?php  $fname = $_REQUEST['fname'];
       $lname = $_REQUEST['lname'];
       echo "Welcome $fname $lname";          ?>
```

serialize.php

2. Add a form and a paragraph containing a span to the body of an HTML document

```html
<form> <input type="text" name="fname" value="Elmer">
          <input type="text" name="lname" value="Fudd">
<input type="button" id="btn" value="Send AJAX Request">
</form>
<p>Output: <span id = "out" ></span></p>
```

serialize.html

3. Now, in the head section of the HTML document, add a script block that specifies an event-handler to send data

```javascript
$(document).ready( function() {

  $( "#btn" ).on( "click" , function() {

    $.ajax( {
      url: "serialize.php" ,
      cache: false ,
      data: $( "form" ).serialize()   ,
      success: function ( msg ) { $( "#out" ).text( msg ) }
    } ) ;
  } ) ;
} ) ;
```

Beware

The **serialize()** method encodes special characters, changing **mike@example.com** to **mike%40example.com** – PHP has a **urldecode()** function to return these.

145

4. Save both documents on the web server, alongside the jQuery library, then push the button to see the response

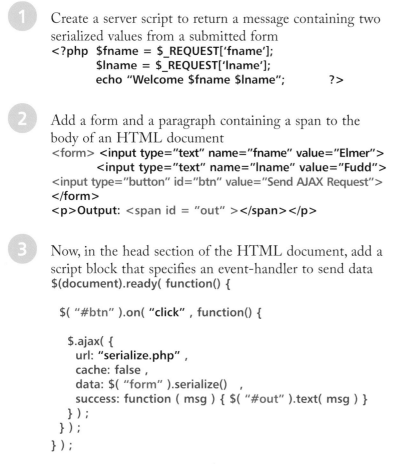

Hot tip

This server script can handle form serialization both as a query string and an array – changing the nominated **data** to **$("form").serializeArray()** produces a like response.

Handling failure

There are in total six ways to make AJAX calls with jQuery. Each of these is demonstrated in the previous examples provided in this chapter and are summarized in the table below:

Method:	Description:
load()	Load content into an HTML element
$.getJSON()	Get data as a JavaScript object
$.getScript()	Get and execute JavaScript code
$.get()	Get data to manipulate in the response
$.post()	Post data for manipulation on the server
$.ajax()	Post and get data with specific options

The first five listed methods often provide sufficient functionality but importantly, unlike **$.post()** or **$.get()**, the **$.ajax()** method provides the ability to execute a function when an AJAX call fails.

Callback functions can be specified to hooks for "Local Events" that get triggered for each AJAX request, including failure:

- **beforeSend** – fires always before the AJAX request begins and can be used to modify the XMLHttpRequest object if required

- **success** – fires only if the AJAX request succeeds, with no errors in the data and with no errors from the server

- **error** – fires only if the AJAX request fails for any reason, so only fires when the success event does not get fired

- **complete** – fires always upon completion, regardless of whether the AJAX request was successful or failed

146

Hot tip

The AJAX request acts like a Deferred object so promise callbacks can additionally be specified by chaining .**done()**, .**fail()**, and .**always()** after **$.ajax()**. In that case, the order of execution is **beforeSend** , **error** or **success** , **done()** or **fail()** then **always()** and finally **complete** at the end.

successfail.php

1. Create a server script to return a message containing a serialized value from a submitted form or an error header

```php
<?php
$num = $_REQUEST['num'] ;
if( is_numeric($num) && ($num < 10) )
echo "Output: $num received" ;
else header('HTTP/1.1 500 Internal Server Error') ;
?>
```

2 Add a form containing a text input, a submit button, and a span to the body of an HTML document

```
<form> <input type="text" name="num">
<br>   <input type="submit">        <br>
<span>Please Enter A Number 1 - 9</span> </form>
```

HTML

successfail.html

3 Now, in the head section of the HTML document, add a script block that specifies an event-handler for the form submission that prevents the default submission action

```
$(document).ready( function() {

  $( "form" ).on( "submit" , function( event ) {

    event.preventDefault() ;
    // AJAX request to be added here.
  } ) ;
} ) ;
```

Hot tip

Notice how the submit event is passed as an argument to the event-handler so its **preventDefault()** method can be called to prevent form submission – so jQuery can submit form data by AJAX instead.

4 Next, in the event-handler block, add the AJAX request to display the result or error without adding it to cache

```
$.ajax( {
  url: "successfail.php" ,
  cache: false ,
  data: $( this ).serialize() ,
  success:  function( result , status , xhr ) {
                      $( "span" ).text( result )  } ,
  error: function( xhr , status , error ) {
                      $( "span" ).text( error )  }
} ) ;
```

5 Save both documents on the web server, alongside the jQuery library, then push the button to see the response

Setting global handlers

In addition to the "Local Events" that are triggered for each AJAX request, described in the previous example, these "Global Events" are also triggered for each AJAX request:

- **ajaxStart** – fires when the first AJAX request begins

- **ajaxSend** – fires just before the AJAX request is to be sent

- **ajaxSuccess** – fires only when the AJAX request completes successfully

- **ajaxError** – fires only when the AJAX request completes with an error

- **ajaxComplete** – fires immediately the AJAX request completes, regardless of success or failure

- **ajaxStop** – fires when all AJAX requests have completed

Event-handlers can be specified for AJAX Global Events by specifying each as an argument to the **ajaxStart(), ajaxSend(), ajaxSuccess(), ajaxError(), ajaxComplete()**, and **ajaxStop()** methods, but only if these methods are attached to the document object:

Hot tip

Global events can also be disabled for a particular AJAX event by setting its **global** triggering option (see page 142) to **false**.

global.html

Don't forget

The file **index.html** should exist by default on the server, so that request will succeed, but the other will fail unless **ghost.html** is added.

1. Add a paragraph containing two buttons and an empty ordered list to the body of an HTML document
```
<p><button id = "good" >Good AJAX Request</button>
<button id = "fail" >Fail AJAX Request</button></p>
<ol></ol>
```

4. Now, in the head section of the HTML document, add a script block assigning a function to a variable that will empty the list and make an AJAX file request when called
```
$(document).ready( function() {

var go = function( file ) { $( "ol" ).empty() ; $.ajax( file ) } ;

} ) ;
```

3. Next, in the script block, add event-handlers for each button to call the AJAX request function
```
$( "#good" ).on( "click" , function() { go( "index.html" ) } ) ;
$( "#fail" ).on( "click" , function() { go( "ghost.html" ) } ) ;
```

4. Then, assign a timer function to a variable that will receive an event, then display that event type and the millisecond portion of the current time when called

```
var at = function( event ) {
  var et = event.type ;
  var ms = new Date().getMilliseconds() ;
  $( "ol" ).append( "<li>" + et +" at "+ ms ) ;
}
```

5. Finally, in the script block, chain event-handlers to the document object for each global AJAX event – calling the timer function and passing their event as its argument

```
$(document).ajaxStart(at).ajaxSend(at).ajaxSuccess(at)
        .ajaxError(at).ajaxComplete(at).ajaxStop(at) ;
```

6. Save the document on the web server, alongside the jQuery library, then push the buttons to see the global events fire in sequence

Beware

You can only append the **ajaxStart()**, **ajaxSend()**, **ajaxSuccess()**, **ajaxError()**, **ajaxComplete()**, and **ajaxStop()** methods after the **$(document)** query – but they can be chained in any order.

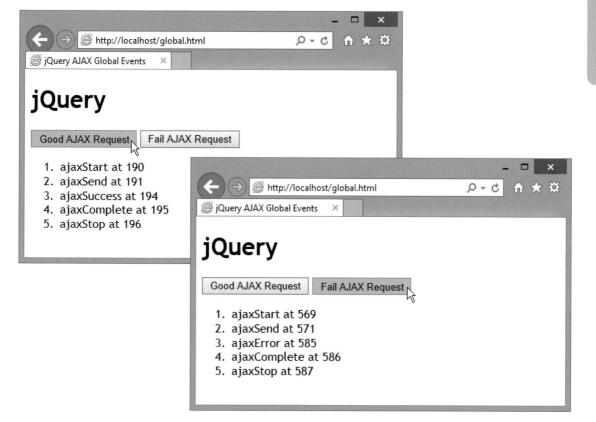

Summary

- Content of an element in a jQuery object can be replaced via AJAX by specifying a URL to that object's **load()** method

- A jQuery selector can be added after a space and the URL argument to the **load()** method to specify a document portion

- Optionally, a callback function can be specified as an additional argument to the **load()** method, to be executed on completion

- A callback function for the **load()** method can receive the returned content, status, and XMLHttpRequest object

- The **load()** method uses the HTTP **GET** and **POST** methods to retrieve data from the server and to send data to the server

- The jQuery **$.get()** method uses the HTTP **GET** method and can accept URL, data, callback, and data type arguments

- The jQuery **$.post()** method uses the HTTP **POST** method and can accept URL, data, callback, and data type arguments

- JavaScript objects can be retrieved by the jQuery **$.getJSON()** method and scripts by the jQuery **$.getScript()** method

- Maximum control when performing AJAX requests is provided by the options of the jQuery **$.ajax()** method

- Form data can be prepared for submission as a string with the **serialize()** method or as an array with **serializeArray()** method

- Unlike **$.post()** or **$.get()** the jQuery **$.ajax()** method provides the ability to execute a function when an AJAX call fails

- Callback functions can be specified as **$.ajax()** options to the AJAX "Local Events" **beforeSend, success, error**, and **complete**

- Event-handlers can be specified to the AJAX "Global Events" **ajaxStart, ajaxSend, ajaxSuccess, ajaxComplete**, and **ajaxStop**

- Global event-handler functions must be specified as arguments to like-named methods attached to the **$(document)** object

9 Using plugins

This chapter demonstrates how to extend functionality of the jQuery library by the addition of plugins.

Grabbing plugins

One of the many joys of jQuery is its flexibility and ability to be extended by additions to its core functionality of "plugin" scripts. These are JavaScript code files that can be easily added to your web page by another **<script>** tag in the document head section, conveniently below the one pointing to the jQuery library file.

The jQuery Plugins Registry is the prime location to grab free plugins online at **http://plugins.jquery.com** listed by category:

1. Open a web browser and navigate to the jQuery Plugins Registry then download a plugin of your choice

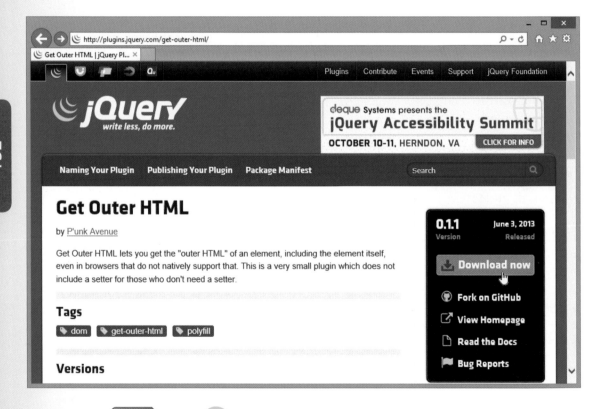

jquery.get-outer-html.js

2. Extract the plugin from the download archive and place it in the directory alongside the jQuery library file

3. In the head section of an HTML document add a tag to include the plugin script below that for the jQuery library
```
<script src="jquery-1.10.2.min.js"> </script>
<script src="jquery.get-outer-html.js"> </script>
```

④ Add a division and a paragraph containing a button and a span to the body of the HTML document

```
<div>Push The Button To Reveal Outer HTML</div>
<p><button id = "btn" >Call Plugin</button>
<hr>Output: <span id = "out" ></span></p>
```

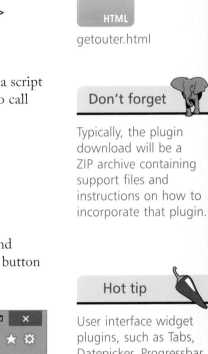

getouter.html

⑤ In the head section of the HTML document add a script block that specifies a button click event-handler, to call the function provided within the plugin script

```
$( document ).ready( function() {

  $( "#btn" ).click( function() {
    $( "#out" ).text( $( "div" ).getOuterHTML() ) ;
  } ) ;
} ) ;
```

Don't forget

Typically, the plugin download will be a ZIP archive containing support files and instructions on how to incorporate that plugin.

⑥ Save the document alongside the jQuery library and plugin file then open it in a browser and push the button to execute the plugin functionality

Hot tip

User interface widget plugins, such as Tabs, Datepicker, Progressbar, etc. can be grabbed from the jQuery UI sub-project at **jqueryui.com**.

153

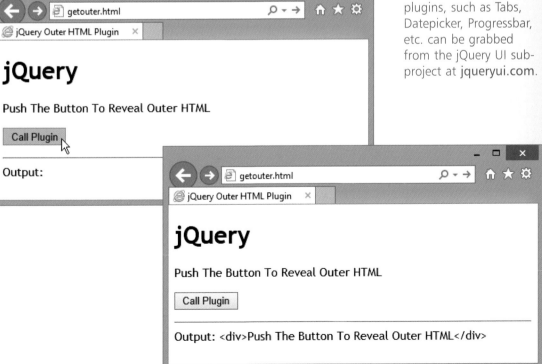

Writing plugins

Just as third-party "plugin" scripts can be included in a web page to extend the functionality of the jQuery library, you can easily create your own plugin scripts to add your very own methods.

Whenever a jQuery selection is made, a jQuery object is returned containing the matched elements and their methods, such as **css()**. The jQuery object gets these methods from its **$.fn** object, which contains all the jQuery object methods. So, in order to provide your own methods, they must be added to the **$.fn** object.

Adding new methods

A method can be added to the **$.fn** object by appending a unique method name, using dot notation, and its functionality can be defined by assigning an anonymous function – with this syntax:

$.fn.*method-name* = function() { *statements-to-be-executed* } ;

The statements contained within a method added to the **$.fn** object can reference the other familiar methods within that same object using the JavaScript **this** keyword. For example, **this.css()**.

Naming plugin scripts

Plugin scripts are simply plain text JavaScript files that contain methods that have been added to the **$.fn** object. The plugin file should adhere to this jQuery plugin naming convention:

jquery.*plugin-name*.js

The plugin file can then be added to your web page by placing another **<script>** tag in the document head section, conveniently below the one pointing to the jQuery library file:

Hot tip

The jQuery **fn** term is an alias for the JavaScript **prototype** keyword – so **$.fn** is simply shorthand for **$.prototype**.

Don't forget

Method definitions are statements, so should end with a ; semi-colon character – this ensures they will work even if the script is compressed.

jquery.basic-plugin.js

basic-plugin.html

1. Create a JavaScript plugin file that extends the jQuery object by defining a new method to set a CSS property
```
$.fn.spotlight = function() {

    this.css( "background" , "silver" ) ;
} ;
```

2. Next, add an ordered list and a paragraph containing a button to the body of an HTML document
```
<ol><li>In<li>Easy<li>Steps</ol>
<p><button id = "btn" >Call Plugin</button></p>
```

③ Now, in the head section of the HTML document, add a style sheet to specify initial rules for the list and its items

```
<style>
ol { width:400px; border:2px dashed gray; }
li { margin:3px; border:2px solid transparent; }
</style>
```

④ Then, in the head section of the HTML document, add a tag to include the JavaScript plugin file

```
<script src="jquery.basic-plugin.js"></script>
```

⑤ Finally, in the head section of the HTML document, add a script block that specifies a click event-handler for the button – calling the method from within the plugin

```
$( document ).ready( function() {

  $( "#btn" ).on( "click" , function() {
   $( "li" ).spotlight() ;
  } ) ;

} ) ;
```

⑥ Save both documents alongside the jQuery library file then open the page in a browser and push the button to see the styles applied by the plugin method

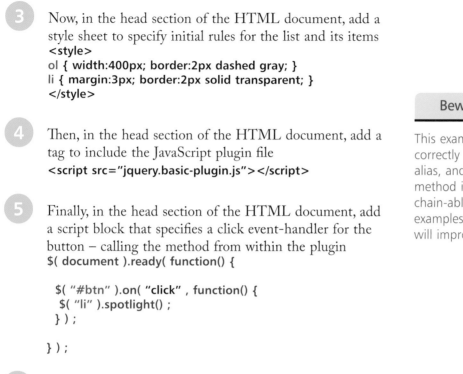

Beware

This example functions correctly but uses the **$** alias, and the **spotlight()** method it defines is not chain-able – subsequent examples in this chapter will improve on this one.

Enabling chains

Building on the previous example, a method defined in a plugin script can be made "chain-able", so other calls can be appended to the caller, simply by returning the jQuery object to the caller.

All that is required to make a plugin method chain-able is the addition of a final **return this** ; statement in its statement block. This is considered good practice and can be found in almost all plugin method definitions:

jquery.chain-plugin.js

1. Create a JavaScript plugin file that extends the jQuery object by defining a new method to set a CSS property
   $.fn.spotlight = function() {

   this.css("background" , "silver") ;

   // Final statement to be added here.
   } ;

2. Now, insert a final statement in the method definition to allow other method calls to be chained to the caller
   return this ;

chain-plugin.html

3. Add an ordered list and a paragraph containing a button to the body of an HTML document
   <ol><li>In<li>Easy<li>Steps</ol>
   <p><button id = "btn" >Call Plugin</button></p>

4. Next, in the head section of the HTML document, add a style sheet to specify initial rules for the list and its items
   <style>
   ol { width:400px; border:2px dashed gray; }
   li { margin:3px; border:2px solid transparent; }
   </style>

5. Then, in the head section of the HTML document, add a tag to include the JavaScript plugin file
   <script src="jquery.chain-plugin.js"></script>

6 Finally, in the head section of the HTML document, add a script block that specifies a click event-handler for the button – calling the method from within the plugin and also chaining a further call to set another CSS property

```
$( document ).ready( function() {

  $( "#btn" ).on( "click" , function() {

    $( "li" ).spotlight() .css( "border","2px solid black" ) ;

  } ) ;

} ) ;
```

Beware

This example functions correctly but uses the $ alias – the next example in this chapter will improve on this one.

7 Save both documents alongside the jQuery library file then open the page in a browser and push the button to see the styles applied by the plugin call and chained call

It is important to recognize that jQuery methods which return something other than the jQuery object, such as utility methods like **height()** (which returns a numeric value), are not chain-able.

Protecting the alias

The previous two examples assume that **$** is an alias to the **jQuery** object but the **$** character may conflict if the plugin gets employed alongside another JavaScript library that also uses the **$** character. To avoid conflict and allow the **$** alias, all code should be enclosed inside a standard "Immediately Invoked Function Expression". This protects the **$** alias and allows the use of private variables – avoiding conflict with like-named variables in other plugins:

jquery.standard-plugin.js

1   Create a JavaScript plugin file that provides an immediately-invoked function block – to protect the **$** alias from conflict and allow the use of private variables
(function ($) {

> // **All jQuery code to be added here.**

> **} (jQuery)) ;**

2   Inside the immediately-invoked function block, insert a method definition block – to extend the jQuery object
$.fn.spotlight = function() {

> // **Method statements to be added here.**
> **} ;**

3   Next, insert statements in the method definition to initialize a private variable and set a CSS property
> **var hue = "yellow" ;**
> **this.css("background" , hue) ;**

4   Now, insert a final statement in the method definition to allow other method calls to be chained to the caller
> **return this ;**

5   Create an HTML document and add a tag in the head section to include the JavaScript plugin file
<script src="jquery.standard-plugin.js"></script>

standard-plugin.html

6   Next, add an ordered list and a paragraph containing a button to the body of the HTML document
<ol><li>In<li>Easy<li>Steps</ol>
<p><button id = "btn" >Call Plugin</button></p>

7 Now, in the head section of the HTML document, add a style sheet to specify initial rules for the list and its items

```
<style>
ol { width:400px; border:2px dashed gray; }
li { margin:3px; border:2px solid transparent; }
</style>
```

8 Finally, in the head section of the HTML document, add a script block that specifies a click event-handler for the button – calling the method from within the plugin and also chaining a further call to set another CSS property

```
$( document ).ready( function() {

  $( "#btn" ).on( "click" , function() {

   $( "li" ).spotlight() .css( "border","2px solid orange" ) ;

  } ) ;

} ) ;
```

Hot tip

You should adopt the plugin format described in this example for ALL your plugins – to protect the jQuery $ alias, to allow private variables, and to enable chaining.

9 Save both documents alongside the jQuery library file then open the page in a browser and push the button to see the styles applied by the plugin call and chained call

standard-plugin.html

jQuery Standard Plugin

jQuery

1. In
2. Easy
3. Steps

Call Plugin

standard-plugin.html

jQuery Standard Plugin

jQuery

1. In
2. Easy
3. Steps

Call Plugin

Passing parameters

When producing plugin scripts it is best to avoid duplicating functionality in methods that perform similar actions. For example, where a **set_red()** method and a **set_green()** method might set the same CSS property with individual values it is more efficient to create a single **set_color()** method that accepts a parameter argument that is the value to be set for that CSS property.

Passing parameters to plugin methods from the caller is more flexible but it is also worthwhile specifying a default value in the method definition so it may be called without parameters:

jquery.param-plugin.js

 Create a JavaScript plugin file that provides an immediately-invoked function block – to protect the **$** alias from conflict and allow the use of private variables
(function ($) {

// **All jQuery code to be added here.**

} (jQuery)) ;

2 Inside the immediately-invoked function block, insert a method definition that accepts one parameter argument
$.fn.spotlight = function(hue) {

// **Method statements to be added here.**
} ;

3 Next, insert a statement in the method definition to initialize a private variable with a passed parameter value or a specified default value
var hue = hue || "yellow" ;

4 Now, insert statements in the method definition to set a CSS property and allow the method to be chain-able
this.css("background" , hue) ;
return this ;

param-plugin.html

5 Create an HTML document and add a tag in the head section to include the JavaScript plugin file
<script src="jquery.param-plugin.js"></script>

6   Next, add an ordered list and a paragraph containing a button to the body of the HTML document

```
<ol><li>In<li>Easy<li>Steps</ol>
<p><button id = "btn" >Call Plugin</button></p>
```

7   Now, in the head section of the HTML document, add a style sheet to specify initial rules for the list and its items

```
<style>
ol { width:400px; border:2px dashed gray; }
li { margin:3px; border:2px solid transparent; }
</style>
```

8   Finally, in the head section of the HTML document, add a script block that specifies a click event-handler for the button – passing a parameter value to the method

```
$( document ).ready( function() {

  $( "#btn" ).on( "click" , function() {
   $( "li" ).spotlight( "aqua" ) .css( "border","2px solid blue" ) ;
  } ) ;
} ) ;
```

9   Save both documents alongside the jQuery library file then open the page in a browser and push the button to see the styles applied by the plugin call and chained call

Hot tip

Remove the parameter value from the caller then reload the page and push the button to see the default color value get applied.

161

Visiting each element

A typical jQuery object contains a collection of HTML elements rather than just one single element. A plugin script can simply manipulate the entire collection of elements, as demonstrated in the previous example, but to manipulate specific elements the plugin can use the **each()** method to loop through the elements.

The results of each iteration of the **each()** method can be returned to the caller to maintain chain-ability, instead of returning the **this** keyword. As the **each()** method is itself chain-able it automatically returns **this** so automatically allows the method to be chain-able:

jquery.each-plugin.js

Don't forget

Remember to specify a default value to the private variable in the method definition – so the method can be called without parameters.

1   Create a JavaScript plugin file that provides an immediately-invoked function block – to protect the **$** alias from conflict and allow the use of private variables
    (function ($) {

    // All jQuery code to be added here.

    } (jQuery)) ;

2   Inside the immediately-invoked function block, insert a method definition that accepts one parameter argument
    $.fn.spotlight = function(hue) {

    // Method statements to be added here.
    } ;

3   Next, insert a method statement to initialize a private variable with a parameter value or a specified default value
    var hue = hue || "yellow" ;

4   Now, insert a method statement to return the result of a function call on each iteration over the collection of elements – allowing the method to be chain-able
    return this.each(function (index) {

    // Function statements to be added here.
    }) ;

5   Then, insert function statements to set a CSS property of a single element on each evenly-numbered iteration
    if (index % 2 === 0)
    $(this).css("background" , hue) ;

6. Next, add an ordered list and a paragraph containing a button to the body of the HTML document

```
<ol><li>In<li>Easy<li>Steps</ol>
<p><button id = "btn" >Call Plugin</button></p>
```

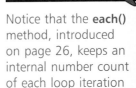

each-plugin.html

7. Now, in the head section of the HTML document, add a tag to include the plugin file and a style sheet for the list

```
<script src="jquery.each-plugin.js"></script>
<style>
ol { width:400px; border:2px dashed gray; }
li { margin:3px; border:2px solid transparent; }
</style>
```

Hot tip

Notice that the **each()** method, introduced on page 26, keeps an internal number count of each loop iteration beginning at zero (even).

8. Finally, in the head section of the HTML document, add a script block that specifies a click event-handler for the button – passing a parameter value for each element

```
$( document ).ready( function() {

  $( "#btn" ).on( "click" , function() {
  $( "li" ).spotlight( "lime" ) .css( "border","2px solid green" ) ;
  } ) ;
} ) ;
```

9. Save both documents alongside the jQuery library file then open the page in a browser and push the button to see the styles applied by the plugin call and chained call

![Two browser windows showing the each-plugin.html page titled "jQuery Each Plugin". The first window displays the heading "jQuery", an ordered list with dashed gray border containing "1. In", "2. Easy", "3. Steps", and a "Call Plugin" button. The second window shows the same page after clicking, with list items highlighted in lime with green borders and a "Call Plugin" button.]

Providing options

Plugin methods can, of course, accept multiple parameters as a comma-separated list of arguments but this can become cumbersome for methods that offer many settings. A better solution is to make the plugin method customizable by accepting an options list within a JavaScript object.

The method can contain an initial list of options, specifying default values, then use the jQuery **$.extend()** method to merge a list passed by the caller. This method accepts a target object as its first argument and an object to merge as its second argument:

jquery.option-plugin.js

1 Create a JavaScript plugin file that provides an immediately-invoked function block – to protect the **$** alias from conflict and allow the use of private variables
(**function ($) {**

// All jQuery code to be added here.

} (jQuery)) ;

2 Inside the immediately-invoked function block, insert a method definition that accepts one options list object
$.fn.spotlight = function(options) {
// Method statements to be added here.
} ;

3 Next, insert a method statement to initialize a variable with a list of default values and another variable merging that list with any list passed by the caller
var defs = { bg: "aqua" , fg: "blue" } ;
var opts = $.extend(defs , options) ;

4 Now, insert a method statement to return the result of a function call on each iteration over the collection of elements – allowing the method to be chain-able
return this.each(function (index) {
// Function statements to be added here.
}) ;

5 Then, insert function statements to set a CSS property of a single element on each evenly-numbered iteration
if (index % 2 === 0)
$(this).css({ background:opts.bg , color:opts.fg }) ;

6 Next, add an ordered list and a paragraph containing a
button to the body of the HTML document
```
<ol><li>In<li>Easy<li>Steps</ol>
<p><button id = "btn" >Call Plugin</button></p>
```

option-plugin.html

7 Now, in the head section of the HTML document, add a
tag to include the plugin file and a style sheet for the list
```
<script src="jquery.option-plugin.js"></script>
<style>
ol { width:400px; border:2px dashed gray; }
li { margin:3px; border:2px solid transparent; }
</style>
```

Hot tip

Remove the options list
from the caller then
reload the page and
push the button to see
the default color values
get applied.

8 Finally, in the head section of the HTML document,
add a script block that specifies a click event-handler –
passing an object with option values and chaining others
```
$( document ).ready( function() {
  $( "#btn" ).on( "click" , function() {
  $( "li" ).spotlight( { bg: "yellow" , fg: "red" } )
        .css( "border" , "2px solid blue" ) ;
  } ) ;
} ) ;
```

9 Save both documents alongside the jQuery library file
then open the page in a browser and push the button to
see the styles applied by the plugin call and chained call

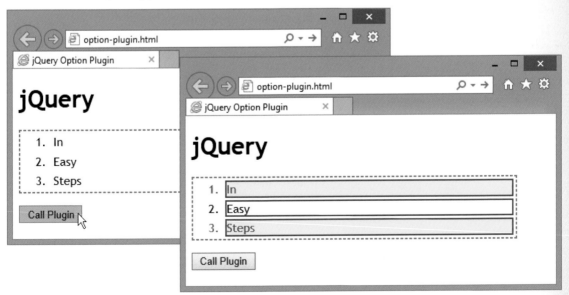

165

Plugging-in dialogs

Putting together some of the techniques demonstrated throughout this chapter, a simple jQuery plugin can be created to produce "modal" dialogs on a web page. The plugin provides a **modal()** method that accepts a Boolean **vis** option, to control the visibility of a modal layer across the entire page, and a string **msg** option to specify a message to be displayed in a dialog box on that layer:

jquery.modal-plugin.js

1 Create a JavaScript plugin file that provides an immediately-invoked function block – to protect the **$** alias from conflict and allow the use of private variables **(function ($) {**

// All jQuery code to be added here.

} (jQuery)) ;

2 Inside the immediately-invoked function block, insert a method definition that accepts one options list object **$.fn.modal = function(options) {**

// Method statements to be added here.

} ;

3 Now, insert method statements to provide options, display a message, determine visibility, and allow chain-ability
```
var opts = $.extend( { vis: true , msg: "" } , options ) ;
$( "#out" ).text( opts.msg ) ;
opts.vis ? this.show() : this.hide() ;
return this ;
```

Don't forget

The **extend()** method merges two objects – in this example the first argument specifies default values and the second specifies any passed option values.

4 Create an HTML document, then add a paragraph containing a button and a division containing a nested division with a button on it to the body section
```
<p><button id = "btn" >Call Plugin</button></p>
<div id = "pop" >
  <div id = "dlg" > <b>Dialog</b>
    <p id = "out" >_</p> <hr>
    <button id = "end" >Close</button> </div>
</div>
```

modal-plugin.html

5 In the head section of the HTML document add a tag to include the plugin file
```
<script src="jquery.modal-plugin.js"></script>
```

6 Next, in the head section of the HTML document, add a style sheet to specify the appearance of each division

```
<style>
#pop { position:absolute; top:0px; left:0px; width:100%;
height:100%; background:rgba(0,0,0,0.3); display:none;
z-index:1; }

#dlg { width:200px; margin:50px auto; padding:5px;
border:1px solid black; background:white; z-index:2; }
</style>
```

Hot tip

Notice that the modal "pop" layer is initially hidden by the style rules but when revealed it has a higher z-index value so features on the page below are unavailable.

7 Finally, in the head section of the HTML document, add a script block that specifies a click event-handler – passing an object with option values and chaining others

```
$( document ).ready( function() {

$( "#btn" ).on( "click" , function() {
        $( "#pop" ).modal( { msg: "That's All Folks!" } )
            .css( "color" , "red" ) ; } ) ;

$( "#end" ).on( "click" , function() {
        $( "#pop" ).modal( { vis: false } ) ; } ) ;
} ) ;
```

8 Save both documents alongside the jQuery library file then open the page in a browser and push the button to see the modal dialog appear with the specified values

Summary

- Plugin scripts are JavaScript files that can be used to extend the functionality of the jQuery library

- The jQuery Plugins Registry offers freely available plugins that can be downloaded for addition to your own web pages

- All methods of a jQuery object are contained in the **$.fn** object

- Additional methods can be appended to the **$.fn** object and can reference other methods in that object by the **this** keyword

- Plugin files should adhere to the jQuery naming convention

- It is good practice to have each plugin method return the jQuery object to the caller so it becomes chain-able

- All plugin code should be enclosed in an Immediately Invoked Function Expression to protect the **$** alias from conflict

- Enclosing code within an Immediately Invoked Function Expression also protects variables from possible conflict

- Plugin scripts should not duplicate functionality

- Methods that allow parameters to be passed to them as arguments are efficient and flexible

- It is worthwhile specifying parameter default values in a method definition so it may be called without arguments

- A plugin method can manipulate the entire collection of elements in a jQuery object or use the **each()** method to manipulate individual elements in turn

- As the **each()** method is itself chain-able it automatically returns the jQuery object so the caller becomes chain-able

- Plugin methods can be made customizable by accepting an options list within a JavaScript object

- The jQuery **$.extend()** method can merge two argument objects into a single object specifying a list of options to apply

10 Handy reference

This section of the book lists the jQuery selectors, properties and methods.

Basic and Hierarchy selectors

Basic:	
("*")	All selector – selects all elements
(".class")	Class selector – selects all elements of the given class name
("element")	Element selector – selects all elements of the given tag name
("#id")	ID selector – selects the single element of the given id attribute
("sel1 , sel2")	Multiple selector – selects the combined results of all given selectors

Hierarchy:	
("parent > child")	Child selector – selects all direct child elements of the given parent
("ancestor desc")	Descendant selector – selects all elements that are descendants of the given ancestor
("prev + next")	Next Adjacent selector – selects all "next" elements immediately preceded by the given "prev" sibling
("prev ~ sibs")	Next Siblings selector – selects all "sibs" sibling elements following the given "prev" element, that have the same parent

Attribute selectors

Attribute:	
[name|="value"]	Contains Prefix selector – selects elements having the named attribute with the given value, or starting with that value followed by a - hyphen
[name*="value"]	Contains selector – selects elements having the named attribute with a value that contains the given value
[name~="value"]	Contains Word selector – selects elements having the named attribute with a value containing the given value word in a space-separated list
[name$="value"]	Ends With selector – selects elements having the named attribute with a value ending with the specified value and matching case
[name="value"]	Equals selector – selects elements having the named attribute with the given value
[name!="value"]	Not Equal selector – selects elements not having the named attribute and elements having the named attribute but not the given value
[name^="value"]	Starts With selector – selects elements having the named attribute and with a value beginning with the given value and matching case
[name]	Has Attribute selector – selects elements having the named attribute with any value

[name="value"] [name2="value"]

Multiple Attribute selector – selects elements having all named attributes with their respective given values

Filter selectors

Basic Filter:	
:animated	Selects all elements currently being animated
:eq()	Selects the element at a specified index number
:even	Selects all elements with an even index number and zero
:first	Selects the first matched element
:gt()	Selects all elements of index greater than a specified index number
:header	Selects all elements that are headers such as h1, h2, h3 etc.
:lang	Selects all elements of the specified language
:last	Selects the last matched element
:lt()	Selects all elements of index less than a specified index number
:not()	Selects all elements that do not match the given selector
:odd	Selects all elements with an odd index number
:root	Selects the element that is the root of the document
:target	Selects the element indicated by the fragment identifier of a URL
Child Filter:	
:first-child	Selects all elements that are the first child of their parent
:first-of-type	Selects all elements that are first among siblings of the same name
:last-child	Selects all elements that are the last child of their parent
:last-of-type	Selects all elements that are last among siblings of the same name
:nth-child()	Selects all elements that are the nth child of their parent
:nth-last-child()	Selects all elements that are the nth child of their parent, counting back from the last element
:nth-last-of-type()	Selects all elements that are the nth child of their parent among siblings of the same name, counting back from the last element
:nth-of-type()	Selects all elements that are the nth child of their parent in relation to siblings of the same name
:only-child	Selects all elements that are the only child of their parent
:only-of-type	Selects all elements that have no siblings of the same name
Visibility Filter:	
:hidden	Selects all elements that are hidden
:visible	Selects all elements that are visible

Content and Form selectors

Content:	
:contains()	Selects all elements that contain specified text
:empty	Selects all elements that have no children, including text nodes
:has()	Selects elements that contain at least one element that matches the specified selector
:parent	Selects all elements that have at least one child, either an element or text node

Form:	
:button	Selects all button elements and input elements of type button
:checkbox	Selects all input elements of type checkbox
:checked	Selects all elements that are checked or selected
:disabled	Selects all elements that are disabled
:enabled	Selects all elements that are enabled
:file	Selects all input elements of type file
:focus	Selects an element that currently has focus
:image	Selects all image elements
:input	Selects all input, textarea, select and button elements
:password	Selects all input elements of type password
:radio	Selects all input elements of type radio
:reset	Selects all input elements of type reset
:selected	Selects all elements that are selected
:submit	Selects all input elements of type submit
:text	Selects all input elements of type text

Core and Callbacks

Core:	
jQuery (arg) and $(arg)	Returns a set of matched elements found in the DOM based on passed argument(s) or created by an HTML string
jQuery.error(msg)	Throws an exception containing the specified message
jQuery.holdReady()	Holds or releases the execution of jQuery's ready event
jQuery.noConflict()	Relinquishes jQuery's control of the $ alias variable
jQuery.support	Contains a collection of properties that represent the presence of different browser features or bugs
jQuery.jquery	Returns a string containing the jQuery version number
jQuery.length	Returns the number of currently matched elements
jQuery.pushStack(elements)	Adds a collection of DOM elements onto the jQuery stack

Callbacks:	
callbacks.add()	Adds one or more callbacks to the callbacks list
callbacks.disable()	Disables the callback list
callbacks.disabled()	Determines if the callback list has been disabled
callbacks.empty()	Removes all callbacks from the callback list
callbacks.fire()	Calls all callbacks with the given arguments
callbacks.fired()	Determines if the callbacks have already been called at least once
callbacks.fireWith()	Calls all callbacks in the list with given context and arguments
callbacks.has()	Determines if a specified callback is in the callback list
callbacks.lock()	Locks the callback list in its current state
callbacks.locked()	Determines if the callback list has been locked
callbacks.remove()	Removes one or more callbacks from the callbacks list
$.Callbacks()	Creates a Callbacks list object

CSS

CSS:	
.addClass(class)	Adds the specified class to each matched element
.css(property)	Gets the value of the specified property of first matched element or sets one or more properties for each matched element
.hasClass(class)	Determines if any matched element is assigned the given class
.height()	Gets the current height of the first matched element or sets the height for each matched element
.innerHeight()	Gets the current height of the first matched element including padding but not border
.innerWidth()	Gets the current width of the first matched element including padding but not border
.offset()	Gets the current coordinates of the first matched element or sets the coordinates for each matched element
.outerHeight()	Gets the current height of the first matched element including padding, border – and optionally margin
.outerWidth()	Gets the current width of the first matched element including padding and border – and optionally margin
.position()	Gets the current coordinates of the first matched element relative to the offset parent
.removeClass(class)	Removes a single class, multiple classes, or all classes from each matched element
.scrollLeft()	Gets horizontal position of the scroll bar for the first matched element or sets the horizontal position of each matched element
.scrollTop()	Gets vertical position of the scroll bar for the first matched element or sets the vertical position of each matched element
.toggleClass(class)	Adds or removes one or more classes from each matched element depending on the class's presence
.width()	Gets the current width of the first matched element or sets the width for each matched element
$.cssHooks	Object that hooks directly into jQuery to override how particular CSS properties are retrieved or set, normalize CSS property naming, or create custom properties

AJAX

AJAX:	
$.ajax()	Performs an asynchronous AJAX request
$.ajaxPrefilter()	Modifies options in readiness to process an AJAX request
$.ajaxSetup()	Sets default values for future AJAX requests
$.ajaxTransport()	Creates an object that handles transmission of AJAX data
$.get()	Loads data from server using an HTTP GET request
$.getJSON()	Loads JSON-encoded data from server using an HTTP GET request
$.getScript()	Loads and executes JavaScript from server using an HTTP GET request
$.param()	Creates a serialized representation of an array or object, which can be used as a URL query string for AJAX requests
$.post()	Loads data from server using an HTTP POST request
.ajaxComplete()	Specifies a function to run when an AJAX request completes
.ajaxError()	Specifies a function to run when an AJAX request encounters error
.ajaxSend()	Specifies a function to run before an AJAX request gets sent
.ajaxStart()	Specifies a function to run when the first AJAX request begins
.ajaxStop()	Specifies a function to run when all AJAX requests have completed
.ajaxSuccess()	Specifies a function to run when AJAX request succeeds complete
.load(url)	Loads data from the server and places the returned HTML into the matched element
.serialize()	Encodes a set of form elements as a string for submission
.serializeArray()	Encodes a set of form elements as an array of names and values

Deferred

Deferred:	
deferred.always(callbacks)	Adds handlers to call when resolved or rejected
deferred.done(callbacks)	Adds handlers to call when Deferred object is resolved
deferred.fail(callbacks)	Adds handlers to call when Deferred object is rejected
deferred.notify(args)	Calls **progressCallbacks** with the given arguments
deferred.notifyWith(context , args)	Calls the Deferred object's **progressCallbacks** with the given context and the given arguments
deferred.progress(progressCallbacks)	Adds handlers to be called when the Deferred object generates progress notifications
deferred.promise()	Returns a Deferred object's Promise object
deferred.reject(args)	Rejects and calls fail callbacks with the given arguments
deferred.rejectWith(context , args)	Rejects Deferred object and calls fail callbacks with the given context and arguments
deferred.resolve(args)	Resolves and calls done callbacks with given arguments
deferred.resolveWith(context , args)	Resolves Deferred object and calls done callbacks with the given context and arguments
deferred.state()	Determines the current state of a Deferred object
deferred.then(callbacks)	Adds handlers to call when the Deferred object is resolved, rejected or in progress
$.Deferred()	Constructs a new Deferred object
$.when(deferreds)	Executes callbacks and returns a Promise object

Effects

Effects:	
.animate(properties , options)	Performs a custom animation of a set of CSS properties
.clearQueue(queue)	Removes from the queue all items that have not yet been run
.delay(duration)	Sets a timer to delay execution of subsequent items in a queue
.dequeue(queue)	Executes the next function on the queue for the matched elements
.fadeIn(duration , complete)	Displays the matched elements by fading them to opaque then calls a function upon completion
.fadeOut(duration , complete)	Hides the matched elements by fading them to transparent then calls a function upon completion
.fadeTo(duration , opacity , complete)	Adjusts the opacity of the matched elements to the specified opacity then calls a function upon completion
.fadeToggle(duration , complete)	Displays or hides the matched elements by animating their opacity then calls a function upon completion
.finish(queue)	Stops the currently-running animation, removes all queued animations, and completes animations for the matched elements
.hide()	Hides the matched elements
.queue(queue)	Shows or manipulates the queue of functions to be executed on the matched elements
.show()	Displays the matched elements
.slideDown(duration , complete)	Displays the matched elements with a sliding motion then calls a function upon completion
.slideToggle(duration , complete)	Displays or hides the matched elements with a sliding motion then calls a function upon completion
.slideUp(duration , complete)	Hides the matched elements with a sliding motion then calls a function upon completion
.stop()	Stops the currently-running animation on the matched elements
.toggle(duration , complete)	Displays or hides the matched elements then calls a function upon completion
$.fx.interval	The rate in milliseconds at which animations fire
$.fx.off	Globally disables all animations

Events

Browser events:	
.resize(handler)	Binds an event-handler to the JavaScript "resize" event or triggers that event on an element
.scroll(handler)	Binds an event-handler to the JavaScript "scroll" event or triggers that event on an element

Document events:	
.ready(handler)	Specifies a function to execute when the DOM has loaded

Event-handler attachment:	
.bind(event , handler)	Attaches a handler to the given event for matched elements
.delegate(selector , event , handler)	Attaches a handler to one or more events for all elements that match the selector, now or in the future
.off(event)	Removes a handler for the given event for matched elements or all their event-handlers if no event is specified
.on(event , handler)	Attaches a handler to the given event for matched elements
.one(event , handler)	Attaches a handler to the given event for matched elements that will only be executed once per element
.trigger(event)	Executes all handlers and behaviors attached to the matched elements for the given event
.triggerHandler(event)	Executes all handlers attached to an element for an event
.unbind(event)	Removes a previously-attached event-handler from the matched elements
.undelegate(selector , event , handler)	Removes a handler from the event for all elements that match the current selector

Keyboard events:	
.keydown(handler)	Binds an event-handler to the JavaScript "keydown" event or triggers that event on an element
.keypress(handler)	Binds an event-handler to the JavaScript "keypress" event or triggers that event on an element
.keyup(handler)	Binds an event-handler to the JavaScript "keyup" event or triggers that event on an element

Form events:

.blur(handler)	Binds an event-handler to the JavaScript "blur" event or triggers that event on an element
.change(handler)	Binds an event-handler to the JavaScript "change" event or triggers that event on an element
.focus(handler)	Binds an event-handler to the JavaScript "focus" event or triggers that event on an element
.focusin(handler)	Binds an event-handler to the "focusin" event. Unlike the "focus" event this supports event bubbling by also detecting the acquisition of focus on parent elements
.focusout(handler)	Binds an event-handler to the "focusout" event. Unlike the "blur" event this supports event bubbling by also detecting the loss of focus on descendant elements
.select(handler)	Binds an event-handler to the JavaScript "select" event or triggers that event on an element
.submit(handler)	Binds an event-handler to the JavaScript "submit" event or triggers that event on an element

Mouse events:

.click(handler)	Binds an event-handler to the JavaScript "click" event or triggers that event on an element
.dblclick(handler)	Binds an event-handler to the JavaScript "dblclick" event or triggers that event on an element
.hover(entry-handler , exit-handler)	Binds event-handlers to matched elements, to be executed when the mouse pointer enters and exits the elements
.mousedown(handler) .mouseup(handler)	Binds an event-handler to the JavaScript "mousedown" or "mouseup" event, or triggers that event on an element
.mouseenter(handler)	Binds an event-handler to be fired when the mouse enters an element or triggers that handler on an element
.mouseleave(handler)	Binds an event-handler to be fired when the mouse leaves an element or triggers that handler on an element
.mousemove(handler)	Binds an event-handler to the JavaScript "mousemove" event or triggers that event on an element
.mouseout(handler) .mouseover(handler)	Binds an event-handler to the JavaScript "mouseout" or "mouseover" event, or triggers that event on an element

Event object:	
event.currentTarget	The current DOM element within the event bubbling phase, typically equivalent to **this** reference
event.data	An optional object of data passed to an event method when the current executing handler is bound
event.delegateTarget	The element where the currently-called jQuery event handler was attached
event.isDefaultPrevented()	Determines whether **event.preventDefault()** was ever called on this event object

event.isImmediatePropagationStopped()
Determines if *event*.**stopImmediatePropagation()** was ever called on this event object

event.isPropagationStopped()
Determines if *event*.**stopPropagation()** was ever called on this event object

event.metaKey	Determines if the keyboard's designated "meta" key (if any) was pressed when the event fired
event.namespace	The namespace specified when the event was triggered
event.pageX	Mouse position relative to the left edge of the document
event.pageY	Mouse position relative to the top edge of the document
event.preventDefault()	Prevents triggering the default action of the event
event.relatedTarget	The other DOM element involved in the event, if any
event.result	The last defined value returned by an event-handler that was triggered by this event

event.stopImmediatePropagation()
Prevents event bubbling by stopping execution of all other event-handlers

event.stopPropagation()
Prevents event bubbling by preventing notification to parent event-handlers

event.target	The DOM element that initiated the event
event.timeStamp	The difference in milliseconds between the time the browser created the event and Epoch at 00:00:00 January 1, 1970
event.type	Describes the type of event
event.which	Indicates the particular key pressed for key events or the particular button pressed for button events

Manipulation

Attributes:

.attr(attribute)	Gets the value of the specified attribute for the first matched element or sets attribute values for every matched element
.prop(property)	Gets the value of the specified property for the first matched element or sets properties for every matched element
.removeAttr(attribute)	Removes the specified attribute from each element in the set of matched elements
.removeProp(property)	Removes the specified property for the set of matched elements
.val()	Gets the current value of the first matched element or sets the value of every matched element

Copying:

.clone()	Creates a deep copy of the set of matched elements

DOM Insertion Around:

.unwrap()	Removes the parents of the matched elements from the DOM – leaving the matched elements in their place
.wrap(element)	Wraps an HTML structure around each matched element
.wrapAll(element)	Wraps an HTML structure around all matched elements
.wrapInner(element)	Wraps an HTML structure around the content of each element in the set of matched elements

DOM Insertion Inside:

.append(content)	Inserts specified content at the end of each matched element
.appendTo(target)	Inserts every matched element at the end of the specified target
.html( )	Gets the HTML contents of the first matched element or sets the HTML contents of every matched element
.prepend(content)	Inserts the specified content at the beginning of each element in the set of matched elements
.prependTo(target)	Inserts every matched element at the beginning of the specified target
.text()	Gets the combined text contents of each matched element (including their descendants) or sets the text contents of the matched elements

DOM Insertion Outside:	
.after(content)	Inserts the specified content after each matched element
.before(content)	Inserts the specified content before each matched element
.insertAfter(target)	Inserts every matched element after the specified target
.insertBefore(target)	Inserts every matched element before the specified target

DOM Removal:	
.detach(selector)	Removes the set of matched elements from the DOM but keeps all jQuery data associated with the removed elements
.empty()	Removes all child nodes of the set of matched elements from the DOM
.remove(selector)	Removes the set of matched elements from the DOM and deletes all jQuery data associated with the removed elements

DOM Replacement:	
.replaceAll(target)	Replaces each specified target element with the set of matched elements
.replaceWith(content)	Replaces each matched element with the specified new content and returns the set of elements that was removed

DOM Element Methods:	
.get(index)	Retrieves one of the DOM elements matched by the jQuery object
.index(element)	Seeks a given element from among the matched elements
.toArray()	Retrieves all the DOM elements contained in the jQuery set as an array

Traversing tree

Traversing tree:	
.children(selector)	Gets the children of each element in the set of matched elements, optionally filtered by a selector
.closest(selector)	For each element in the set, gets the first element that matches the selector by testing the element itself and traversing up through its ancestors in the DOM tree
.contents()	Gets the children of each element in the set of matched elements, including text and comment nodes.
.each(function)	Iterates over a jQuery object, executing a function for each matched element
.find(selector)	Gets the descendants of each matched element filtered by a selector, jQuery object, or element
.next(selector)	Gets the immediately following sibling of each element in the set of matched elements. If a selector is provided, it retrieves the next sibling only if it matches that selector
.nextAll(selector)	Gets all following siblings of each element in the set of matched elements, optionally filtered by a selector
.nextUntil()	Gets all following siblings of each element up to but not including the element matched by the selector, DOM node, or jQuery object passed
.offsetParent()	Gets the closest ancestor element that is positioned
.parent(selector)	Gets the parent of each matched element filtered by a selector
.parents(selector)	Gets ancestors of each matched element filtered by a selector
.parentsUntil(selector)	Gets the ancestors of each matched element, up to but not including the element matched by the selector, DOM node, or jQuery object
.prev(selector)	Gets the immediately preceding sibling of each element in the set of matched elements, optionally filtered by a selector
.prevAll(selector)	Gets all preceding siblings of each element in the set of matched elements, optionally filtered by a selector
.prevUntil(selector)	Gets all preceding siblings of each element up to but not including the element matched by the selector, DOM node, or jQuery object
.siblings(selector)	Gets the siblings of each element in the set of matched elements, optionally filtered by a selector

Traversing filtering

Traversing filtering:	
.add(elements)	Adds elements to the set of matched elements
.addBack(selector)	Adds the previous set of elements on the stack to the current set, optionally filtered by a selector
.end()	Ends the most recent filtering operation in the current chain and returns the set of matched elements to its previous state
.filter(selector)	Reduces the set of matched elements to those that match the selector or pass the function's test
.first()	Reduces the set of matched elements to the first in the set
.has(selector)	Reduces the set of matched elements to those that have a descendant that matches the selector or DOM element
.is(arg)	Checks the current matched elements against a selector, element, or jQuery object and returns true if the argument matches
.last()	Reduces the set of matched elements to the final one in the set
.map(callback)	Passes each element in the current matched set through a function, producing a jQuery object containing the return values
.not()	Removes elements from the set of matched elements
.slice(start , end)	Reduces the matched elements to a subset at the specified indices

Data

Data:	
.data(key , value)	Stores data at each matched element or returns the value associated with the key at the first matched element
.removeData(key)	Removes data previously stored with .data() associated with the specified key at matched elements
$.data(element, key, value)	Stores jQuery data at the specified element or returns the value associated with the key at the specified element
$.removeData(element , key)	Removes jQuery data previously stored with $.data() associated with the specified key at the specified element
$.hasData(element)	Determines if the specified element has jQuery data previously stored with $.data()

Utilities

Utilities:	
$.contains(container , contained)	Determines if a DOM element is a descendant of another DOM element
$.extend(object1 , object2)	Merges two objects together into the first object
$.fn.extend(function)	Extends the jQuery prototype object to provide new methods that can be chained to the **$()** function
$.globalEval(code)	Executes some JavaScript code globally
$.grep(array , function)	Finds array elements that satisfy a filter function
$.inArray(value , array)	Returns index number of first occurrence of given value in array (or -1 if not found)
$.isArray(object)	Determines if given object is an array
$.isEmptyObject(object)	Determines if given object is not enumerable
$.isFunction(object)	Determines if given object is a JavaScript function
$.isNumeric(value)	Determines if given value is a number
$.isPlainObject(object)	Determines if given object is a plain object created using "{}" or "new Object"
$.isWindow(object)	Determines if given object is a window
$.isXMLDoc(node)	Determines if given node is in an XML document
$.makeArray(object)	Converts an array-like object into a true array
$.map(array , callback)	Translates all items in an array or object to new array
$.merge(array1 , array2)	Merges two arrays into the first array
$.noop()	Executes nothing but useful as a placeholder
$.now()	Returns a number representing the current time
$.parseHTML(string)	Parses a string into an array of DOM nodes
$.parseJSON(json)	Parses a JSON string into a JavaScript object
$.parseXML(string)	Parses a string into an XML document
$.proxy(function , context)	Returns a new function with the particular context
$.trim(string)	Returns a copy of the given string with all whitespace removed from the beginning and end
$.type(object)	Determines the JavaScript class of the given object
$.unique(DOM-element-array)	Sorts an array of DOM elements in place and removes any duplicates that are the exact same node